Supernanny

How to Get the Best from Your Children

Jo Frost

HYPERION

New York

JO'S ACKNOWLEDGEMENTS

So many people have helped this book happen. I'd love to be able to thank you all individually, but there are too many names! Where would I begin?

So, a big, big thank-you to everybody who worked so hard on *Supernanny* at Ricochet Productions, to the creative crew who photographed, assisted and designed the book and to the gang at Hodder for delivering it.

A special thank-you to the families that made the series happen, to the families over the years that I've worked with, and to MY family and friends—you know who you are! —who have supported me and then some.

And last, but not at all least, I'd like to thank Sue Ayton and Liz Wilhide for helping me find my voice.

ISBN 0-4013-0810-4

Hyperion books are available for special promotions and premiums. For details contact Michael Rentas, Manager, Inventory and Premium Sales, Hyperion, 77 West 66th Street, 11th floor, New York, New York 10023, or call 212-456-0133.

FIRST EDITION

Designed and typeset by Smith & Gilmour, London

10 9 8 7 6 5 4 3 2

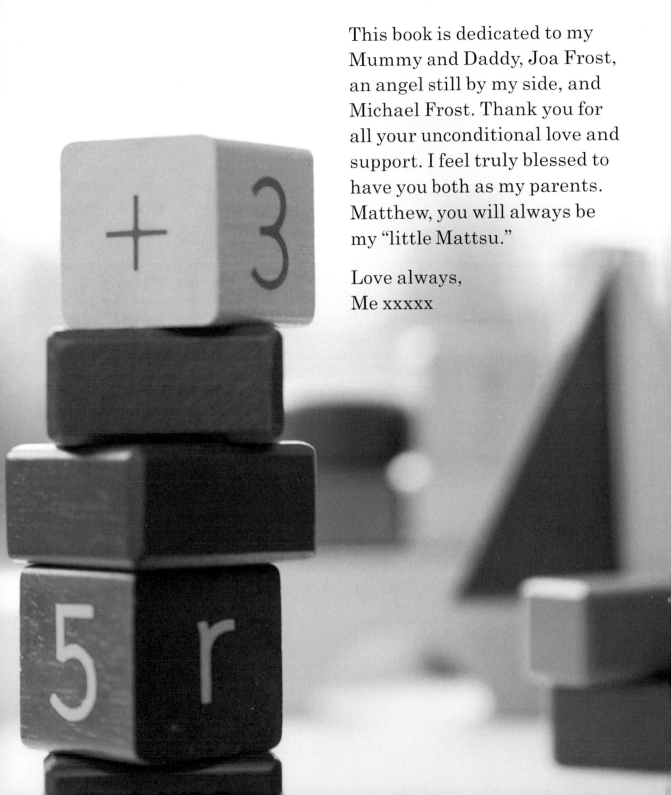

This book is dedicated to my Mummy and Daddy, Joa Frost, an angel still by my side, and Michael Frost. Thank you for all your unconditional love and support. I feel truly blessed to have you both as my parents. Matthew, you will always be my "little Mattsu."

Love always,
Me xxxxx

CONTENTS

Introduction

One day not so long ago, when I was nanny to two little girls, we all went out to the park. It was a hot day and the girls were wearing bandannas to keep the sun off their heads. After we had been playing for a while, a woman came over to me. "How did you manage to do that?" she asked in amazement. "How did you get them to keep their bandannas on?" I looked at her and lowered my voice to a whisper. "*Superglue.* Just a little line across the forehead." Judging by her horrified expression, I think she believed me for a fraction of a second. Then she realized I was joking!*

Needless to say, you won't find any techniques involving superglue in this book. You won't find anything that will harm children in any way—physically, mentally or emotionally. What you will find are commonsense ways of dealing with the type of ordinary challenges and problems most parents of children under five face most days of the week. I didn't invent the techniques. I suspect no one single person could put their hand on their heart and claim to have invented them out of the blue. By and large I've simply followed my instincts and observed parents and kids to see what worked and what didn't work. What I've called the "Involvement Technique," for example, is just what many parents have done instinctively over the years when they have needed to get on with a household chore. The "Naughty Step Technique"—a way of enforcing a rule by getting a child to think about their behavior—has probably been around as long as stairs have had steps and rooms have had corners.

I didn't wake up one morning and decide to be a nanny; it just happened. But if I stop and think about it, my first ever Saturday job was in a maternity shop, so it's not surprising I've ended up working with children!

I love meeting different people and I love children. My parents would always joke that I was a real chatterbox when I was a child —and it seems nothing's changed! Mummy and Daddy were always being introduced to new people when we were on vacation because I made friends with their kids first. When I got older, I did a lot of baby-sitting and a bit of part-time nannying. I got my first permanent job after answering an ad posted up on a bulletin board in a bookshop.

Fifteen years later, I've had a lot of hands-on experience. I've been a permanent nanny, a temporary nanny, and a troubleshooting nanny. I've gone on holidays with families, moved home with them and even moved continents with them. I've looked after children ranging in ages from a few hours old to fourteen. I've answered countless calls from worried parents at 2 A.M., and from worried friends of those families I've worked for. Since the first series of the television program *Supernanny*, I've been overwhelmed with letters from people I've never met who have tried the techniques featured on the program and wanted to tell me how things have turned around for them. It's just wonderful to hear from them and get that positive feedback.

Some of those letters point out that I'm not a parent. That's true. I'm not a pediatrician, either, or a child psychologist. I've had no formal training to do what I do. Which puts me in much the same position as most parents, without the intense emotional attachment (although we nannies have feelings too!).

The big difference is that I've had many years of experience looking after all sorts of children at all stages and I'm not meeting these challenges for the first time. I've seen children through weaning and toilet training, teething, tantrums and the first day at school. Along the way I've observed behavior, listened to other people talking about child care issues and, most importantly, I've listened to my own gut instincts.

Quite early on, I worked out that nannying isn't just about looking after kids and nursery duties. In some ways, you are the bridge between the child and the parent. It puts you in the unique position of observing how families work. It's a dynamic that constantly fascinates me—the way everything is linked and related. You can see this clearly if you're in an objective position, without the tug on the heartstrings. The trouble is that when many parents find themselves in difficulties, they're too emotionally involved to see the bigger picture.

This book is a way of helping parents step back and see the bigger picture. It's what I do on *Supernanny* when I'm working with individual families who've become troubled—simply because they've unknowingly allowed themselves to get trapped in a pattern that is sending them around in the same old negative circles. I don't think there's such a thing as a "bad" child. I believe that every child has the potential to behave as expected. By that I don't mean Goody Two Shoes. I mean happy, relaxed children who have their own individual characters but who know where the limits are.

Everything I've seen and experienced convinces me that children need boundaries. And to keep those boundaries in place, there needs to be discipline. Discipline is not about harsh punishment. A key part of it, in fact, is praise. But it does mean setting rules and backing up the rules with firm and fair control.

A lot of parents find it hard to discipline their kids. It could be that they fear their children won't love them anymore. The result is that they let their kids take charge when they're not equipped to do that. And when you're a child, being in charge is a confusing and unhappy place to be.

Imagine walking into a bank to pay a check and you're asked to step into the manager's shoes. Without the training, without working your way to the top, you wouldn't have the first idea what to do. It's the same with kids. Kids who find themselves in charge are in a situation that they mentally just cannot handle.

I had a secure, loving upbringing. I was blessed with parents who gave me self-belief and told me the world was my oyster. Neither of them ever broke a promise to me. My mother was an inspiration. She taught me so much without my even realizing I was being taught. My father made me feel safe—the world couldn't touch me. If I was worried about something, we would talk it through and he would reassure me. At the same time, though, my parents insisted on standards, on showing respect and on manners, in the way we all behaved both to each other and to other people. But I was still a child. I could get mucky, dirty and have fun like all kids, without the worries of the world resting on my shoulders.

Parenting is hard these days. Our society has changed. When I was a child I could go to the park with my brother Matthew without my parents being overly worried. People didn't even lock their doors where we lived. Now parents worry all the time. Every day there are scare stories in the media about what's dangerous or harmful for children; the next week those same reports are contradicted. It makes it difficult to know where you stand. At the same time, it seems being a parent has become so competitive. It's hard to relax and trust your instincts when other parents are constantly telling you how advanced and well-behaved their kids are.

In the past, there were often grandparents and other family members nearby who could lend a hand and give support and advice. Many parents today find that they have none of these traditional support systems in place. When both parents work, that means more stress and isolation. When there's just one parent coping with kids on their own, it's even harder.

Some people naturally take to parenting like ducks to water. Some don't. It's just something else that has to be learned, understood and practiced. The more you know, the more you read and talk to people, the more you will trust yourself, find your own feet and make your own choices. Be confident. How you bring up your kids is your choice—it's up to you.

Raising your children is the most important role you will ever have. You are literally giving them strong foundations for life. But it doesn't have to be a slog. Parenting can and should be a joy.

When the opportunity came along to get involved in *Supernanny* (through another ad, this time in a magazine), I saw it as a chance to put across some ideas and messages that I felt strongly about. We made the pilot, which involved showing a single parent how to get to grips with her four children. Together we worked through techniques on discipline, management and praise. These techniques worked. The result was one contented mom and four happy, manageable kids. Two weeks later I found myself with a television series.

For me, *Supernanny* has been and continues to be a wonderful chance to share the experience and lessons I've learned from working with families. It has also been a chance for me to give that something back.

Enjoy your children.

* ...So how *do* you get a child to keep her hat on? It's easy.
When she takes it off, you tell her to put it back on. She takes it off.
You tell her to put it back on. She takes it off. You tell her to put it back on.
She takes it off. You tell her to put it back on. She takes it off.
You tell her to put it back on. She takes it off. You tell her to put it back on ...

MY TOP TEN RULES

IF I COULD SUM UP MY APPROACH TO CARING FOR CHILDREN, THESE WOULD BE MY TOP TEN RULES. THEY'RE BASED ON OBSERVATION, NOT ON THEORY. THEY APPLY TO MOST SITUATIONS YOU'RE GOING TO FACE, AND YOU'LL FIND THEM SUMMARIZED AT THE END OF EACH CHAPTER IN THE SECTION ON TROUBLESHOOTING, WHERE I'LL BE MORE SPECIFIC ABOUT HOW THEY APPLY IN DIFFERENT CASES.

1. PRAISE AND REWARDS

The best rewards are attention, praise and love. Sweets, treats and toys are not necessary as rewards. A star chart or a special outing can back up a pattern of good behavior.

2. CONSISTENCY

Once you have made a rule, don't change it for the sake of a quiet life or because you're embarrassed. Make sure that everyone—which includes caregivers and your partner—keeps to the same rules as well. A rule is a rule is a rule.

3. ROUTINE

Keep your home in basic order and maintain a routine. Set times for waking, meals, bath and bed are the cornerstones of family life. Once a routine is in place, you can be a little flexible, if you're on vacation, for example. It's a framework, but it doesn't have to be rigid.

4. BOUNDARIES

Children need to know there are limits to their behavior—which means what is acceptable and what is not. You need to set rules and tell them what you expect.

5. DISCIPLINE

You can only keep the boundaries in place by discipline. This means firm and fair control. It may just take an authoritative voice and a warning to get the message across. Otherwise, there are other techniques you can use, none of which involve punishment.

6 WARNINGS

There are two kinds of warning. One tells a child what's coming next—you're the Speaking Clock telling her that bathtime is coming up soon, or that you're getting near to putting her lunch on the table. The other is a warning for bad behavior. That gives her the chance to correct her behavior without any further discipline.

7 EXPLANATIONS

A small child can't understand how you want him to behave unless you tell him. Show and tell to get the message across. Don't reason or make it too complicated—just state the obvious. When you are disciplining a child, explain why in a way that is appropriate for his age. Ask him if he understands the reason why he has been disciplined so that the message hits home.

8. RESTRAINT

Keep cool. You're the parent and you're in charge. Don't answer a tantrum by a display of anger or respond to shouting by shouting back. You're the adult here. Don't let them wind you up.

9. RESPONSIBILITY

Childhood is all about growing up. Let them. Allow them to do small, achievable things to boost their self-confidence and learn the necessary life and social skills. Get them involved in family life. But make sure your expectations are reasonable. Don't set them up for failure.

10. RELAXATION

Quality time is important for everyone, including yourself. Let your child unwind at bedtime with a story and cuddles. Make sure you, your partner and your other kids have quality time for individual attention.

Ages and stages

The first five years of childhood are a time of rapid change on all fronts—physically, mentally and emotionally. The physical milestones are easy to spot. In what seems like the blink of an eye, the beautiful little bundle you brought home from the maternity ward sits up, crawls, then takes his first tottering steps. Before long, he's mountaineering over the side of his crib and getting into everything.

What's going on inside your child's head is every bit as dramatic, though far less obvious. Between birth and five years old, she will make huge advances in the way she understands the world and relates to those around her.

"Isn't Jemima walking yet? Molly walked at nine months."

There's enough competitiveness attached to parenting these days without me adding to it. The point of this chapter is not to burden you with anxiety if your child is not meeting a particular "target" or to suggest you give yourself a pat on the back if he is miles ahead. It's simply to show what you can realistically expect from each stage. Or, more importantly, what you shouldn't expect.

Knowing what makes your child tick will help you adjust your parenting skills to suit her stage of development. Time after time in my work I've seen parents trying to "reason" with a child who is simply too young to follow a logical conversation. I've seen toddlers asked to choose between a huge range of options when they have next to no means of making those kinds of decisions.

Once a child starts to talk, it's surprising how quickly parents seem to forget that they are not dealing with a pint-sized, wayward adult but with someone whose take on the world is still very basic. Just as you wouldn't expect a six-week-old baby to pull herself to standing, you shouldn't expect a two-year-old toddler to have the social and mental skills of a child twice her age.

All this has a direct bearing on how you look after your kids. Understanding how children change and grow—inwardly as well as outwardly—helps every parent meet their child's needs in the right way and in their own time.

The new baby: birth to six months

A newborn baby has no idea what a person is. He doesn't yet know that the person who is holding him is his mother, or that the person holding him is separate from him at all. But he is tuned right in to the sight of your face, the feeling of being held, the sound of your voice. That's because deep down he knows his survival is going to depend on getting his needs regularly met by someone else. Which means you.

Studies have shown that babies can hear in the womb, and it is thought that they may even recognize their mother's voice from birth. For mothers, on the other hand, it takes a while to recognize their child's cry and even longer to work out what that cry means. Hunger? Gas? Tiredness? What no mother would deny is that crying works. That's because it's supposed to.

The early months are a steep learning curve. If it's your first baby, you're going to feel a bit like you're on a roller coaster—high as a kite one minute, all at sea emotionally the next, pretty tired most of the time. What's most important about this stage is not how expertly you can change a diaper but that you keep on responding to your baby's needs, and that you get your own needs met, too.

You cannot spoil a baby. Contrary to what your mother or grandmother may tell you, your baby is too young to be "wrapping you around her little finger"—that delightful stage is yet to come! By responding to your baby when she cries, you are not "giving in" to her, you are giving her tender loving care. Each time you do, she learns to trust that her needs will be met in the future.

Leaving a young baby to cry for long periods in the first four months of life doesn't teach him to wait a bit longer for a meal, until the time is more convenient for you. It doesn't teach him that he doesn't need another cuddle. It doesn't teach him to go back to sleep. It teaches him that there is no one out there who cares, and that there's nothing he can do about it.

In the same way, discipline has no role at all in the early months. That is not to say that babies do not benefit from the reassurance of routine. The early weeks may show very little consistency when it comes to eating and sleeping patterns. By three to six weeks you'll probably find that things have become much more predictable.

You can't force a two-month-old baby into a routine when it comes to sleeping, but you can ease her into a feeding routine. Start by observing how much milk your baby takes. If she cries after a meal, she might be a hungrier than average baby and need more. Between three to six weeks, as babies take more milk, most fall into a pattern of wanting to eat every two to four hours.

Now you've got a choice here. You can go with the flow, or you can use that pattern to develop a routine. It's up to you. But remember, as a parent, you have more control over the situation than you think. If your baby seems to be wanting to eat at the same times each day, but those times mean you are awakened often during the night, you can shift things along by feeding her slightly earlier than usual, until the intervals are easier for you to cope with. Sometimes if you give a breastfed baby a bottle at 11 P.M., she can hold out until 4 A.M. before she needs another.

Babies need a lot of physical care from the word go—feeding, changing, bathing, soothing. But they also need stimulation. They can't talk yet, but they love to hear your voice and watch your face. Keep communicating, and before very long you'll be rewarded with the first smile. A short while after that will come the first babbling sounds as your baby "talks" back, imitating the sounds you have made to her.

NEW BABIES REALLY ENJOY:

- Loads of kisses

- Close physical contact—cuddling, carrying, back-rubbing and massaging

- Watching faces—in the early weeks, the human face is the best toy of all.

- Rocking and rhythmic jiggling

- Music and the sound of your voice

- Colorful patterned objects at a fairly close range, particularly those that move

COPING STRATEGIES:

- Take every chance you can to rest. Sleep while the baby's sleeping.

- Keep things ticking over, but don't expect to achieve domestic perfection.

- Enlist help from your partner, friends, mother—anyone who can share the load of cooking, shopping, and so on.

- Set aside at least some time for your significant others—your partner and other children—to nip in the bud any feeling of resentment or jealousy.

- Share baby duties—bathing, burping, diaper changes.

- Feel human again. Pamper yourself. Get your hair done.

The older baby: six months to 18 months

Enormous changes have taken place in the first six months. Your helpless infant has become a baby who can hold his head up, roll, grab a toy, smile, laugh, babble and recognize Mom, Dad, brothers and sisters, and other familiar faces. He will have started on his first solid food; he may be taking drinks from a cup. The second half of the first year, your baby really begins to explore the world.

During this stage, physical development is pushing forward to that first tottering step, which often occurs sometime around or before the first birthday, and nearly always by 18 months. Increasing mobility, by rolling and crawling, means your baby no longer has to wait for the world to be brought to her; she can go and look for it herself. And when she finds it, she usually puts it in her mouth. If you haven't done so already, now's most definitely the time to think about child-proofing your home and being extra careful with hygiene—see Action Stations, page 42.

Every day your baby will seem more like a little person, with his own likes and dislikes and with his own individual character. Feeding and sleeping should be much easier; if not, there are strategies you can adopt that are featured elsewhere in this book. But what you should bear in mind is that until your child is at least a year old, he is still a baby. When he cries, he's letting you know he needs something or that something has upset him—or maybe it's just that you've told him "no." You can't "spoil" him at this stage, any more than you can spoil a newborn.

Babies of this age sometimes get into things they shouldn't. A baby pulls a cup off a shelf because a) he can and b) no one stopped him. He doesn't pull a cup off a shelf to annoy you or defy you or because he is naughty. It's just where his mission to explore has taken him that day. "Look! A smooth blue thing! Let's put it in my mouth and see what it is. Oops. Too heavy! Where's it gone?"

You can't use discipline on a ten-month-old baby, but you can and should warn her not to do something. Use a firm, low voice to say "No" or to warn her not to touch. You can also explain why. "That's hot." She won't understand the words, but she'll respond to your tone and it will get you into the habit of explaining, which will become much more important later.

In many ways, this is a delightful age; in other ways, it can be pretty testing. You have to keep a step ahead of the game; eyes in the back of the head come in handy. You'll be able to get less done while your baby is awake because she's more mobile—and she'll be awake for longer. During this time, you'll also notice that your baby needs increasing attention from you in the form of play. She can't yet do much by herself, but she's old enough to get bored when she isn't getting enough stimulation. Putting her in a playpen with plenty of toys and something to look at can help to ease the strain for short periods. But don't dump the baby in a playpen or crib when you're angry or fed up or when she's crying—she'll come to associate it with bad feelings.

TEETHING

If boredom is a new reason for crying at this age, so is teething. Just when you congratulated yourself on getting into some kind of routine, here comes the tooth monster to upset the apple cart. The first tooth, which appears around six months, usually comes as much as a surprise to the parents as it does to the baby. After you've got through the first bout of teething, you'll know how to spot the signs the next time. And the time after that.

Once the first tooth is cut, the key is knowing when a child is teething, when she's sick and when she's just having an off-day. If her temperature is very high or she has other signs of illness, you need to take her to the doctor without delay. If she's just fretful and shows no other signs, she's probably not teething.

SIGNS OF TEETHING:

- Red cheeks. I call this "X's and O's" cheeks, because the redness often shows up as fine red crisscross lines.

- Drooling

- Biting down hard on everything

- Small white clear bubbles on the gums

- A slight temperature, raised by no more than a degree. If the temperature goes up, seek medical attention.

- Smellier diapers than usual—the smell is unmistakable

- Sometimes a diaper rash

- Fretful crying and waking in the night—teething hurts!

- Slight loss of appetite

REMEDIES:

- Hard teething rings. Some can be frozen for extra relief.

- Herbal teething powders

- Mild sedatives to take away the pain

- Plenty of comfort and empathy

SEPARATION ANXIETY

Another feature of this stage is that the baby will generally show signs of becoming even more attached to his mother, preferring Mom above everyone else. This often takes the form of protest or distress when Mom leaves the room or even when she moves toward the door. As long as your baby can see you, he's happy, but as soon as he can't, he begins to cry. Children vary as to how clingy they are and how long this stage lasts, but it generally peaks at about nine months and trails off gradually afterward, reappearing again at 18 months. It's often called "separation anxiety," and it's thought to be a sign that the baby is now old enough to remember and compare. He knows you're leaving and he knows he's not going to like it when you go, because he didn't like it the last time.

When you can't even go for a pee without triggering a bout of wailing, you may find that your patience becomes as strained as your bladder. If you have arranged to go back to work during this period, you may find that your plans are at odds with this particular stage of development.

EASING SEPARATION ANXIETY:

★ Make sure your child is not ill or under emotional stress. Children can also get clingy for those reasons.

★ Accept that it's a stage and it will pass. The worst time for separation anxiety will be before the first birthday.

★ Don't allow yourself to get angry or feel trapped. Take a deep breath when you start to feel overwhelmed or stressed.

★ If you have to leave the room quickly for a short period, keep chatting to your baby to let her know you're still around.

★ Don't vanish when she's not looking.

★ If you need to leave your child with a caregiver during this period, make sure she gets to know that new person well first. It will help her to settle in.

★ Reassure your partner that he hasn't done anything wrong and the baby is not taking sides! Dads can feel left out when separation anxiety is at its worst. They also need to know that this will pass, and that there are other ways they can help.

★ I like to play peekaboo games with young children. It helps to teach them that what they can't see is still there. I might pull a sheet over my head or get on the bed and cover my whole body with the blanket. With older children, I'll make balls disappear under cups. If you can make it fun and make them laugh, they learn much more quickly.

The toddler: 18 months to three years

After a child has taken his first step, things will have started to get even more interesting. He will have been launched like a NASA probe into a whole new stage of mobility. All sorts of things will have become much more fun to play with, not to mention to take to bits. Full speech will still be some way off, but by 18 months he may be saying a few recognizable words. One of which will almost certainly be "no."

Which brings us to the really interesting part. From now until around three years old, your child is officially a "toddler." She's no longer a baby, but she doesn't have anything like the skills, physical, mental or social, that she'll have by her first day at school. Like the teenager, she's somewhere in between. And sometimes that's a nice place to be and sometimes it isn't—for you and for her. That gives us another first. The First Tantrum.

Unlike the previous stage, when the world was a wonderful, surprising thing to explore, the toddler rapidly discovers that the world—and that includes you—often exists simply to prevent him getting what he wants when he wants it: which is NOW. He has new physical freedoms he's just itching to try out. For the first time, he's getting an idea of what it's like to be a little individual with a will of his own. The problem is that he's not yet equipped to be one. For a very good reason: the part of the brain that will eventually give him self-control is not yet fully developed. Although he's striving for independence, he's still very dependent on you.

Even if your toddler is talking a mile a minute and seems to be understanding what you say, his mind works very differently from yours. Up until two and a half at the earliest, there are a number of key things that he just can't do or understand.

Toddlerhood, which used to be called the "Terrible Twos," has stages of its own. When it begins, generally before two, your child will have next to no control over her impulses and will often be frustrated by her own inabilities or by the world around her. As it comes to an end, around about three or slightly later, she will have matured to the point that you can expect some self-control. Not much, but some.

Toddlerhood is challenging. But it doesn't even have to be a bad time if you approach it with sensible expectations. Toddlers can be irritable, illogical, exhausting and unpredictable. But they can also be funny, loving, enthusiastic and full of life. Enjoy this time while you can.

WHAT MAKES TODDLERS TICK:

★ Patience is not a toddler virtue. Some toddlers can hang on for a bit, but many can't wait—not even for a minute.

★ He can't plan ahead. If he has an impulse, he'll act on it and he won't have the first idea where that's going to take him or what he'll feel like when he gets there.

★ He can't control himself.

★ He has no sense of danger.

★ His memory is limited. That means you're going to have to repeat yourself. Over and over.

★ He doesn't understand what a promise is until it's delivered. When he wants something, he wants it right away. His mind will be set on one thing. That means you can't bargain with him. Or you can try, but you'll lose.

★ He can't cope with too many choices. He simply doesn't understand what "either...or" is all about. A lot of things he'll say he wants will be contradictory. He'll want his shoes on and he'll want his shoes off—at the same time.

★ He can't understand that his actions may affect other people's feelings. He doesn't want to take turns. If you say, "Let Susie have the toy for a little while," he'll think the toy has gone for good. Cue explosion.

★ He wants more attention than it is humanly possible to give, and he wants it for longer than there are hours in the day.

COPING STRATEGIES

Reasoning, pleading, bargaining, threatening—none of these work with this age group. For these strategies to work, your child would need mental powers she just does not yet have.

Setting boundaries, firm and fair control and routine do work. As soon as toddlerhood sets in, your child will do everything in her power to rule the roost and get her own way. At times it might seem to you like she is forever having a mad moment—usually after she's knocked another toddler down at playgroup and you're dying of embarrassment. But she isn't being malicious and she isn't being aggressive on purpose. She is resorting to physical behavior because she can't verbally resolve what she's feeling.

That doesn't mean you should give in or turn a blind eye. Nor does it mean you should try to turn back the clock and stamp on all attempts at independence, however messy and time-consuming they are. At this stage it doesn't matter if your child covers his face, the table and the floor with dinner in his attempt to feed himself. It does matter if he's using the full range of toddler weapons— screaming, kicking, throwing tantrums—to turn the household upside down and impose his will. What he needs now are clear boundaries and the sense that there's something bigger out there that he cannot control—which is you.

Consistency starts to become a real issue at this time. Before, if your child noticed any differences in the care she received, she wouldn't have known how to turn that to her advantage. Now, however, she will sense that there is much mileage to be gained by "divide and rule." "Divide and rule" is one of the first manipulation strategies that young children master. They learn this one fast. If you don't present a united front, or if you change your tune according to how strong you're feeling on any given day, your toddler will find that chink in your armor like a heat-seeking missile.

TANTRUMS

Your child is very unlikely to get through toddlerhood without erupting in one of those spectacular floor shows that is also known as a tantrum. Some children are more prone to tantrums than others; they seem to have a shorter fuse. Perhaps it's just something in their makeup.

The tantrum is where the toddler comes up bang against the world and the world doesn't budge. It can be triggered by many different things, but the root cause is always some form of frustration. Either your child has found she can't do something that she wants to do because she doesn't yet have the necessary skills to do it, or something hasn't turned out the way she expected, or you have stopped her from doing something she wants to do, or tried to make her do something she doesn't want to do—or she has simply got to the end of her emotional tether. Whatever the reason, the fuse is lit and everything blows.

It's bad enough when the tantrum happens on the living room floor. But it can just as easily happen at the supermarket, in the car, at a friend's house, in front of your parents… or any other place where it's going to be a million times more excruciating.

You can minimize the frustration your child encounters at this age, but you can't get rid of it completely: it's built into the learning process, and your child is at the stage where he is wired to learn. Involvement techniques and similar strategies outlined in the chapter Setting Boundaries (page 58) can sometimes head a tantrum off at the pass. But not always.

What you mustn't do once the tantrum has started is give in. Giving in to a tantrum is the best way of ensuring that there will be plenty more where that one came from. You've just proved that it worked.

Once a child is in the throes of a full-blown tantrum, it's pretty terrifying—for you and for her. She has literally "lost it" and is absolutely flooded with feelings of rage. Some children run around screaming, some fall on the floor kicking and yelling, some will headbutt the furniture or even you.

Here's how to deal with a tantrum:

- The first thing to do is to make sure she can't hurt herself, hurt other people or damage things.

- Try to stay calm. Anger will only inflame the situation. If you can't guarantee you'll keep your temper, leave the room. The worst thing you can do is have a tantrum back.

- Forget about trying to reason with her. She can't hear you (and doesn't want to).

- Some children come out of a tantrum more quickly if they are held securely. With others, that makes it worse.

- Remove yourself from the room—if you can —once you are sure she's not going to hurt herself or damage anything. If the tantrum is semi-deliberate, as it can be when an older toddler wants her way, removing attention completely can do the trick.

CLINGINESS

The drive to independence is a powerful process that pushes the toddler forward. At the same time, he can be surprisingly clingy. This is not a time when he will separate easily from you. He's unlikely to wail every time you leave the room, unlike the nine-month-old, but he'll be keen to know that you're around and won't like being left with someone else he doesn't know or trust very well.

Although your child won't necessarily cry when you leave the room, she may well cry, scream and generally kick up a fuss when you go out and leave her with a babysitter. Some children react so badly and get so hysterical that parents abandon a social life altogether rather than go through the experience again. Sometimes the child's anxiety seems to transfer itself to the parents, so they become unusually worried that something will happen when they are out of the house.

Here's how to cope:

★ Use a sitter that your child knows and likes. Don't spring a stranger on him.

★ Ask the sitter to come early so that your child can get into a fun activity before you leave.

★ Explain calmly that you're going out and that you'll be back.

★ Give him a kiss and a cuddle and say, "See you later."

★ Leave promptly.

★ Remind yourself that the tears will probably be over by the time you've turned the corner.

★ Repeat this during the daytime, too, at a friend's house, so your child can see the pattern.

TOILET TRAINING

Timing is everything when it comes to toilet training. It's a big mistake to start too early—it always leads to problems later on. There's a very good reason why you shouldn't even think about toilet training before two or two and a half. Before 18 months, a child is physically incapable of controlling his bowels or bladder. It takes longer for him to understand cause and effect. When a child is ready, both physically and mentally—which may not be until the age of two or three—toilet training can often be easy and quick.

See Toilet Training, page 104.

The preschooler: three to five

Toddler behavior doesn't magically go away at three; in fact, many experts consider children as old as four still technically to be toddlers. Self-control comes gradually and tantrums may lessen because a child can reason better, but they won't disappear completely. The maturing process can also be upset by the arrival of a new brother or sister. Suddenly that sensible little four-year-old vanishes and you've got your irrational toddler back again.

But somewhere between three and five, toddlerhood begins to wane. The brain is now more developed. There's an increase in self-control and less acting on impulse. Your child is learning to think and beginning to play with other kids rather than simply alongside them. He can wait (a little). Altogether he's less wrapped up in his own little world and beginning to realize that other people live in it too.

This is the age of constant questions. Speech development varies, but by the age of three, many kids can express themselves pretty clearly. If the two-year-old's favorite word was "No!," the three-year-old's is "Why?" Kids at this stage not only ask a lot of questions, they love to challenge you and get involved in conversations. But a full grasp of reasoning is still some way off. Don't expect them to follow a logical argument or a detailed explanation. When a three-year-old wants her way, "Why?" is just a more sophisticated version of "No!" This becomes obvious when you've given her an explanation and it promptly leads to another "Why?"

A young child's powers of reasoning being what they are, many find it difficult to separate truth from fiction, or fact from fantasy. Whatever pops into his head somehow becomes true. Around the age of four, an "imaginary friend" can appear out of the blue and hang around for a while. Often that imaginary friend will have similar likes and dislikes: "Binky doesn't like peas either." Sometimes "Binky" will be blamed when the child has done something wrong.

Make-believe, tall tales and imaginary friends don't mean your child is developing into a liar; it's just a normal stage of development and a sign of an imagination in overdrive. Without directly challenging the child or denying his very real feelings, you can start to introduce him gently to the difference between what is true and what isn't. Teach him that it's good to tell the truth and take responsibility for what he does, and not blame others —even imaginary others—all the time.

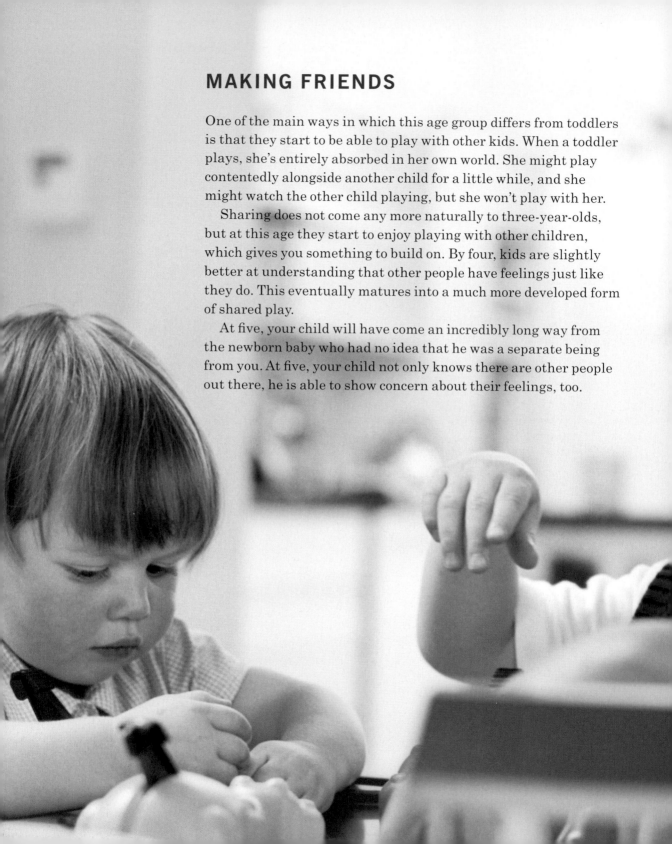

MAKING FRIENDS

One of the main ways in which this age group differs from toddlers is that they start to be able to play with other kids. When a toddler plays, she's entirely absorbed in her own world. She might play contentedly alongside another child for a little while, and she might watch the other child playing, but she won't play with her.

Sharing does not come any more naturally to three-year-olds, but at this age they start to enjoy playing with other children, which gives you something to build on. By four, kids are slightly better at understanding that other people have feelings just like they do. This eventually matures into a much more developed form of shared play.

At five, your child will have come an incredibly long way from the newborn baby who had no idea that he was a separate being from you. At five, your child not only knows there are other people out there, he is able to show concern about their feelings, too.

He understands rules and can follow them. He can take turns; he can control his behavior to some degree; he can think about what will happen if he takes a particular course of action. He's capable of understanding when you reason with him. That's a long way in five years—and he's only just getting started.

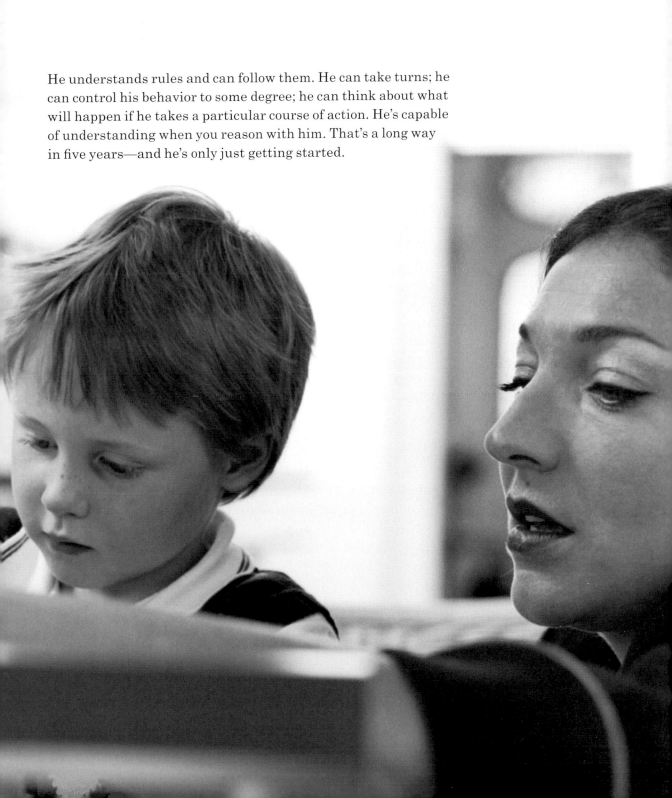

Action stations

One of the most important ways you can protect your junior stuntman or stuntwoman is to toddler-proof your home. This has the added advantage of saving your sanity. If your home is full of potential hazards, you won't be able to turn your back for a second. If there are precious things within reach, you won't be able to relax. The same is true when there are surfaces and finishes that can't take a beating—or a spill of juice—without permanent damage.

A fully toddler-proofed home would probably bear some resemblance to a padded cell full of toys. That's not practical or desirable. Kids have to learn to respect their surroundings, and you should not have to descend to their level simply to survive the preschool years. But you'll need some kind of avoidance strategy— it will save unnecessary conflict, help prevent accidents and save you money on repairs and replacements, as well as time and effort on clearing up.

When you look around your home, there are the obvious accidents waiting to happen—breakable things at low level, trailing wires inviting a little someone to give them a sharp tug, household cleaners and chemicals in unlocked cupboards. But until you're a parent you might not fully appreciate the strange workings of the toddler mind. Get down on your knees and try to see the world from their height.

For example, children often go through a stage when they are fascinated by keys. Keys fit into locks. Locks look a bit like sockets. Sockets are down at toddler level. Do keys go into sockets—let's see! That's why the socket cover was invented.

Or what about the video recorder? Wouldn't it be a good idea to mail a slice of toast and jam in that slot there?

Not all small children are daredevils and not all are mindlessly destructive. But every child tries something completely bonkers (at least to the adult mind) at least once and at some stage all seem to find breaking things to bits irresistible. At the same time, while young children may have tons of energy and newfound physical skills, their bodies are under imperfect control. They have accidents; things break. That's life.

BE SAFE:

* Many toddlers love to climb, and they will climb up things without the slightest idea how they will get down, or that they are in any danger of falling, or that falling might hurt. They'll climb curtains, they'll move chairs and use them like ladders. All of the interesting things are happening several feet above their head: you can't really blame them. Keep climbing opportunities to a minimum. Don't put obviously tempting things like sweets out on open view on upper shelves. If you have bunk beds, make sure the younger ones are on the bottom, with a secure railing on top. Bookcases should be firmly anchored to the wall so there's no risk of them toppling over.

* Anything that trails down from above is just inviting a toddler to pull it to see what's on the other end. You won't be able to avoid trailing power cords in every situation, but keep your eyes peeled. Turn pan handles away from the edges of burners and use the rear burners, if you can.

* Useful child-safety devices include window locks or grills, socket covers, corner protectors for the sharp edges of tables and counters, non-slip bath mats, childproof locks for household cupboards where cleaning products, medicine, chemicals and alcohol are stored, smoke alarms, stair gates and safety film for French doors, picture windows and other expanses of glass.

* Another useful device is a wire tidy that neatly packages the cabling from TVs, DVDs and video recorders.

* You'll save yourself time, effort, expense and heartache if you move your treasured possessions out of toddler-reach. You don't want to be saying "don't touch" 35,000 times a day. That's not fair on your children, either. It's their home, too.

* Washable covers for sofas and chairs, washable rugs and washable curtains make it easier to deal with the after-effects of sticky little fingers. Scotchgard your fabric.

* Don't think about investing in surfaces and finishes that need constant upkeep to look good. Spending the extra time on maintenance will only annoy you and may deprive your children of time you could be spending with them.

* Your home may feel safe and secure. But remember: most accidents happen there, not in the world outside, where you're more likely to be on your guard.

Routines
and rules

I'm a firm believer in the benefits of routine for young children. A routine provides a clear structure for daily life. It also allows you to arrange things so that everyone gets some quality time for themselves.

Small children function best when things are predictable and when more or less the same things happen at the same time each day. There are good reasons for this. If you don't have a set time when your child goes to bed, for example, sometimes you will be trying to put her to bed when she's not tired, and at other times you'll be trying to put her to bed when she's overly tired. You will think she's acting up when what she really needs is sleep. A child's bedtime is too important a part of their day and has too much of an effect on everyone else in the household to be left to such a hit-and-miss approach. In the same way, many parents don't realize that moving mealtimes around drastically or leaving too long a gap between them can play havoc with their child's blood sugar levels, leading to mood swings and unnecessary tiredness.

A routine will help you meet your child's physical needs at the right time—food when she's hungry, bed when she's tired. Set times for key activities are essential. Going through the same stages every day also means that a child knows what to expect. Without a clear routine, when basically anything could happen at any time, kids start to feel insecure and jumpy. No wonder—you're always catching them on the run. When they're always expecting the unexpected, they can't settle and relax. They may meet each change of activity with defiance or a tantrum because they aren't mentally prepared for it. A routine, on the other hand, allows you to ease them through the stages, telling them what's going to come next, so they don't feel rushed or surprised.

Routines build consistency into family life. You also need an agreed-upon set of rules. Before you can insist on certain standards of behavior from your child, you have to decide what is acceptable and what is not. Then you have to stick to your guns. If you're always bending the rules or moving the goalposts, your child won't have the first clue what he should be doing and won't take you seriously. "Will I get in trouble for this or not?" Most of the time, when rules are always changing or not being consistently enforced, your child will see that as a golden opportunity to do exactly what he wants.

How to work out a timetable

Modern life is hectic enough as it is. When you've got small children, you may begin to think there are simply not enough hours in the day for anyone's needs to be met, least of all your own. The answer is to prioritize.

As soon as parents start feeling pressured for time, several things tend to happen. They cut back on their own quality time —time they spend on themselves or with each other. They cut back on the time they spend with their older kids. And they try to cut corners by rushing their toddlers from pillar to post. The result is that no one's happy.

When you haven't enough time for yourself or enough time alone as a couple, resentments build up and marriages are put under strain. When your older children don't feel they're getting enough attention, they often blame their younger brothers and sisters and become jealous of them, or they may act up in different ways just to remind you that they're there. And, at best, a rushed toddler who feels you're being too abrupt with her will dig in her heels; at worst, you'll have a tantrum on your hands.

Working out a timetable or household routine allows you to juggle everyone's needs and interests, as well as to give your toddler the clear framework he needs to feel secure. Some parents don't like the idea of a routine because they think it's too rigid. But a routine actually allows more room for fun because it removes so much of the stress you get when you are trying to manage limited time. When one activity doesn't eat into the time allocated for another, no one loses out. Suddenly everything won't seem so rushed and chaotic. Suddenly you'll find you have breathing space again. You'll feel on top of life, not squashed under the pressure of it.

On *Supernanny,* we write out each family's routine and household rules and stick them on the fridge. You don't have to do that. Just find the pattern in your own family, memorize it and keep to it as much as you can.

SCHEDULING TIPS:

★ Mealtimes and bedtimes are the cornerstones of your routine. I'm in favor of early mealtimes for small children— 5:00 to 5:30 for the evening meal.

★ The point of the routine is to help you get things achieved within a reasonable length of time. If getting your toddler from bath to bed, for example, takes too long, it will eat into your evening. If you don't allow enough time, your child will find it harder to wind down. Children can always sense when you're rushing them.

★ Don't be too rigid. If you slacken the reins by half an hour here and there, it won't make a lot of difference.

★ Be realistic. If your child is always slow in getting dressed, allow enough time for that. Don't make it more difficult for yourself.

★ In summer, you might want to move bedtime to half an hour later. Children find it difficult to get to sleep when it's still light.

★ Allocate special times for every child to have individual attention, and rotate these between each parent. One day, it's Mom's turn to bathe the toddler and Dad's turn to read him a story and put him to bed; the next day, it's the other way round. If that isn't possible, make sure you take turns on the weekend.

★ Include quality time for yourself and your partner. This is not an optional extra. It's a necessity. You should want that. Don't you?

TALKING THEM THROUGH IT

Once you have drawn up a timetable—whether it's just in your head or written out and stuck on the door of the fridge—you have to talk your child through it. Every day. And at every stage of the day.

Younger children have shorter attention spans because they don't remember things for very long. They can't tell the time. They can't read the routine that you've put on the wall, and they certainly can't read your mind. A routine will only work if it's backed up verbally, over and over. Otherwise, each shift from one activity to the next will still come as a surprise. You know it's bathtime in five minutes' time, but your child won't know that unless you tell him.

You may find yourself starting to sound like the Speaking Clock, but this is a really important part of making a routine work. Don't be irritated by the sound of your own repetitive voice. Give clear, calm and repeated warnings in an everyday tone about each new activity, with a few minutes between warnings. This gives a young child who thinks largely in terms of "now" a chance to get ready for what's coming and to feel involved in the way the day's turning out. This will make her much less likely to dig in her heels or to try to control things herself.

"In five minutes, we're going to the park. Let's go and find your shoes." Be excited at the prospect. Children are very receptive to the tone you use.

"Mom's getting the towel now. In two minutes, it'll be time to get out of the bath."

You're talking them through their day. But what you're not doing is offering them lots of choices. It's "Let's put on your shoes," not "Will you put on your shoes?" or, even worse, "Which shoes do you want to wear?" It's okay to offer a toddler a choice between two acceptable alternatives. But offering a toddler lots of choices tells him that you don't know what you're doing—otherwise, why are you asking?—and that therefore he's the boss.

The same thing is true of bargaining. Don't say, "If you put on your shoes, you can go to the park." Say, "When we've put on your shoes, we'll go to the park." The difference in the way you say things may be very subtle, but the differences in the results are not.

Taking the time to speak to your child in this way will save you a great deal of time and effort in the long run. When parents are busy, they have a tendency to speak to their kids in stressed-out tones and give them instant cut-off points—"Bed. Now!"—which leaves no room to maneuver, and backs a child into a corner. To a child, a stressed voice equals panic. Children very quickly pick up the signs that you are frazzled, and most react by trying to take advantage of the situation—with another tantrum, if it comes to that. Staying calm and taking the time to warn them about what's coming next lets them know that you're in charge.

A CALM AMBIENCE

A settled routine takes the chaos out of everyday life by allowing you to manage your time properly. As soon as you introduce a routine, things should start to get a lot calmer all round.

You can also help keep things on an even keel by making sure things are reasonably tidy. If everything's in a mess, you'll waste a lot of time turning the house upside down just to find your child's pajamas or shoes. Chaos also winds kids up and teaches them that they don't have to respect their surroundings. The problem, of course, is that they're responsible for most of the chaos. See page 153 for ways of coping with mess.

Excessive noise levels can also upset small children, even if they're the ones doing most of the shouting and screaming. Don't add to the volume unnecessarily by turning up the TV or blasting out music from the radio.

Around the age of a year to 18 months, many children develop an abrupt fear of loud noises. Vacuum cleaners, food processors and fireworks are some of the things that can set them off. This is usually short-lived, but in the meantime you might have to choose your moment to switch on the juicer. I once looked after a little girl who was very scared of the blender. I used to pop her on the sofa about ten feet away, warn her that I was going to use the blender, quickly switch it on and off a couple of times so she could get used to the idea—and then use it. The nearer a child is to the source of the noise, the more she will panic.

Rules

Imagine playing a game where everyone else knows the rules except you. You couldn't possibly join in. It would make you pretty frustrated.

Now imagine playing a game where the rules keep changing.

"When you pass GO, you get $200."

"When you pass GO, you pay $200."

"When you pass GO, nothing happens."

You'd soon invent your own rules. You'd try to participate by whichever means you could.

Kids are just the same. If you don't tell them the rules—what you expect them to do—they can't begin to abide by them. If you tell them a rule and then change it when you're challenged, they won't take you seriously. If you set impossible rules they simply can't follow, you're looking at endless and needless strife. And that's unfair to your child.

GET REAL

Rules are boundaries that children need. But the rules not only need to be consistent, they also need to reflect what you can realistically expect your child to achieve at that particular age. For example, it's pointless to expect a toddler to tidy up like an adult—all his programming is driving him in the direction of what you call chaos and mess. The answer is not to set a tidiness rule you have no chance of enforcing, but only to allow him to play with messy materials under supervision—if he can get his hands on the Magic Markers when your back is turned, you have only yourself to blame if the walls are then covered with his "artwork."

One of the most common mistakes that parents make is to expect levels of understanding from their kids that are well beyond what they are capable of. But the reverse can also be true. Sometimes a parent will still think of their child as a little baby and treat her as such long after she has moved on from that stage. Parents can find it hard to see babyhood go, particularly if it's their youngest and last child. Other parents may baby a child because it makes looking after her easier to manage.

It may seem like yesterday since you brought her home from the hospital, but at two or three years of age, your child needs to be handled in a very different way from an infant. She will be desperate to try things out for herself and hugely resistant if you persist in babying her by not allowing her to attempt simple tasks such as feeding herself. She'll be too little to do that neatly, but you'll save yourself unnecessary conflict if you let her express her independence in ways that don't harm anyone. She needs to learn. Don't suppress that.

Don't expect perfection. Work with what you've got. Get real and you won't be setting your child up for failure.

BE CONSISTENT

Many parents make up the rules as they go along. That's okay—in some circumstances you have to. The problem comes when parents don't consult each other about the rules they set. The result is often inconsistency. It's worth making some time to sit down together and discuss a common approach. What type of behavior do you both consider unacceptable? What are you prepared to be more relaxed about? Where do you differ? It is essential to reach an agreement so that you have one set of house rules that everyone can follow. If Mom and Dad don't present a united front, children very quickly learn to play one off against the other emotionally.

When you and your partner have very different ideas about how you expect your kids to behave, it will quickly become impossible to enforce any rules at all—good, bad or indifferent. Talking things over can help to air what lies behind your different approaches. It may be that you were brought up in a stricter household than your partner, or vice versa. That might never have mattered until now. But the arrival of a child can reveal differences between you and your partner that you were not aware of before. Whatever your individual expectations, now's the time to sort them out and come up with a shared approach.

The parent who is with the child most of the time may have a better idea of what that child is capable of understanding, and therefore which rules are most appropriate for that particular age group. At the same time, that parent may be too worn out by the ceaseless demands of a toddler to see the wood for the trees and spot how that child is walking all over them. Open the lines of communication and keep them open, so you not only deal with the current situation but are also able to anticipate the changes to come.

UNACCEPTABLE BEHAVIOR

There are certain types of behavior that are always beyond the pale. Your child may yet be too young to understand the reasons why, but she needs to be shown, clearly and firmly, that there are some things she is not allowed to do. The "strictly forbidden" category includes behavior that hurts other people—hitting, biting, punching, pushing, name-calling—and behavior that could endanger the child herself— such as unbuckling her seatbelt or not holding your hand when crossing a road. When a child is very young, such behavior is largely thoughtless and impulsive, but as soon as she shows signs of doing it on purpose, firm and fair control and enforcement of the rules are required. If you don't teach your child not to hit you or her brothers and sisters, she will think she can hit strangers or other children outside the home. It's a moral issue.

LESS IS MORE

When it comes to household rules for young children, a few clear rules are better than too many. If you have a rule about simply everything, you'll spend more time policing your kids than parenting. A small child can't tell the difference between an important rule— "hitting people is wrong"—and a petty one—"keep your mouth closed when you're chewing." When he's very small, forget about minor misbehavior and focus on the big stuff. Constantly bringing your kids up short takes all the fun out of family life and heightens tension. Toddlers get frustrated enough in the daily course of events; don't pile on the opportunities for more frustration, or you'll have a real battle on your hands.

As children get older, you can develop a new level of rules once they have mastered the one before. Move with your child as he develops.

Working with other caregivers

Clear guidelines—a daily routine and agreed-upon house rules—help a great deal when you are sharing the care of your children with others. Not only do Mom and Dad have to work together and follow more or less the same agenda, so should grandparents, babysitters, au pairs and nannies.

Before you leave your children in the care of other people, spend some time explaining what should happen when and what sort of behavior you do and don't allow. Kids get confused when they are exposed to different ways of doing things all the time. Grandma may be much stricter than you and a stickler for manners, or she might be much more lenient, happily indulging her grandchildren in a way she would never have done when you yourself were small. You need to explain how you do things so your child stands a chance of staying on an even keel.

At the same time, allow each person to develop their own special relationship with your child, as long as what they do doesn't undermine your efforts. A grandparent often enjoys the role of being a softie, and few can resist slipping their grandchildren a few treats. Don't rob them of that—they've earned it, after all.

Leaving your child for a short while in the care of other people is one thing, but if you need to return to work and the arrangement is more permanent, a shared understanding of the basic rules and routines is essential. Parents, particularly working mothers, often experience strong feelings of guilt when they leave their children in the care of others. Sometimes that results in a relaxation of the rules on the part of the parent when they come home from work. But you aren't doing your child any favors if you indulge him in an attempt to overcome your own guilty feelings. He needs quality time with you when you come home, but he doesn't need to have the rulebook thrown out of the window. He will feel much happier and much more secure if he senses that everyone who looks after him does so in the same way. When a parent relaxes the rules, it's also unfair on the caregiver, who will have to pick up the pieces the next day. Make sure you allow enough time to have a chat about what happened during the day.

Coping with disruption

No matter how organized you are and how smooth your daily routine is, there will be times when things are less predictable. Some types of disruption are unavoidable—illness and bouts of teething fall into this category. Other types of disruption are either avoidable or you can take steps to lessen their impact.

Routines don't have to be set in stone. It's fine to relax the routine a little on the weekend and allow your children to stay up a bit later on Saturday night. Just be prepared to be strong on Sunday.

Avoid scheduling potentially disruptive events when they could have a specific effect on your child's routine. For example, don't invite guests over at a time that might interrupt kids' meals or bedtimes. Small children find it difficult to separate from their parents or to forgo their attention, and some are very shy of people they haven't met before or don't know very well. If something out of the ordinary is coming up, take the time to explain to your child what's likely to happen.

Routines often go out of the window on holidays. Two weeks away is not a huge break when you're an adult, but for a small child, it might as well be a lifetime. If you abandon a routine completely on holiday, you're going to have your work cut out when you get home. Going on holiday can throw your child's sleeping habits out of kilter or even introduce a sleeping problem when none existed before. The solution is not to stay at home, but to plan in advance how you can stick to the routine. Mealtimes and naptimes should be kept consistent as far as possible.

AWAY FROM HOME:

Recognize that if you choose a far-flung holiday destination, you are going to have to deal with the disruption that comes from long periods in transit, as well as jet lag if there's a major shift of time zone. Young children suffer from jet lag just as do adults. They will need a few days to adjust.

Keep to the key times in your routine as far as possible—waking, meals, bath and bedtime are the cornerstones of the schedule. Activities and location are inevitably going to be different, and that's enough change for most kids to cope with.

If it's hot, expect your child to want to eat less. Don't make an issue of it, and remember to offer her plenty of water.

Take comforters, toys, and reminders of home to help your child settle into a different bed. If there's something she really likes to eat, you might consider taking a supply of it with you. Always take medication, basic remedies and formula with you in case you can't get it at your destination.

Setting
boundaries

Routines and household rules are important for small children. Making sure that basic structure is kept in place means discipline.

From how much TV should be allowed, to questions of diet and nutrition, almost any issue remotely connected with kids and their care has a tendency to spark off a heated debate in the media. But discipline is one area of family life that is absolutely guaranteed to arouse controversy.

What's too strict? What's not strict enough? I could sit and debate the issues all day long. But I do know one thing. Parents lose their authority when they bend over backward to try to become their kid's best buddy. Discipline is about finding that balance where you are warm with your children, but you're firm when you need to be. That means there has to be respect on both sides.

If you're too tough on your kids, you'll run the risk of breaking their spirit. But if you don't set any limits at all, you'll end up with kids who don't know how to control themselves. Sooner or later—generally at school—those children will face a situation outside the home where that lack of self-control is going to result in an even bigger problem. It might affect the child's ability to learn; it might make it hard for her to make friends.

You might think that a child who is allowed to do exactly what he wants, when he wants, would be happy

and carefree. But that's not the case. A child who gets away with everything thinks that he's in charge. When you're a toddler, that's a confusing idea. Too much freedom doesn't tell a child that you love him so much you want him to have anything and everything; instead, it tells him that you are not bothering to show him where the limits are. Children who go undisciplined are often frightened, insecure, angry, confused and unhappy. They have no idea whatsoever where they're going, and that upsets them. When they get what they want, or what they think they want, they are still not content, but keep on pushing at the boundaries to see if there's anything at all you're prepared to stop them from doing or having.

In the first series of *Supernanny*, I visited a family where the head of the household was two and a half years old. Charlie was literally ruling the roost. If Charlie made the whole family—Mom, Dad and his two older siblings—sit in the dark with the TV off and the heat off, that's what the family did. Charlie was getting his way all the time, every day, but that didn't make him happy. The more his parents gave in to him, the more he screamed and yelled. After we introduced a few basic techniques of discipline, along with a new routine, an agreed-upon set of household rules, and plenty of praise and encouragement, Charlie was a changed child. Instead of the angry little boy who hadn't the first idea what to do with the freedom he had been given, he was relaxed, happy and secure, knowing he could participate in family life without running the show.

You wouldn't give your car keys to your toddler and expect her to drive to go shopping. But you are doing something rather similar if in the course of everyday life you let her dictate who does what, when, where and how. Just as she's some years away from taking her driving test, she doesn't yet have the reasoning powers or the common sense to run her own life— not to mention yours.

In my experience, many parents who start out imposing no rules at all often wind up changing their minds somewhere down the line when things are getting really out of hand. Then they find they don't have many techniques at their disposal. Once a pattern of bad behavior has been established, it takes effort to change it. But, surprisingly, it can be done without too much grief. Then it's not just the Charlies of this world who become happier and more relaxed. Everyone else in the family benefits, too.

Finding the right approach

All children have their own characters that are obvious from the word go. There are the lively ones, who don't sleep much and who are tuned into everything that's happening around them. There are the laid-back ones, who go with the flow, and the ones who are more strong-willed. You can't predict what sort of child you will have, but you can adapt your methods to deal with the new person who has arrived in your life. Some won't need as much firmness as others. But please remember that discipline is not about stomping on your child's personality, breaking her spirit or trying to turn her into someone she's not. The whole point is to allow kids to be themselves within the limits of acceptable behavior.

You stand a better chance of success if you are comfortable with the style of discipline you adopt. But if you're one of those parents who find it hard to take charge at all, this is not to say that you should forget about discipline altogether! There are a number of different techniques outlined in this chapter, and you might find some of them work better for you than others. Don't give up if a technique feels a bit unnatural at first. Parenting sometimes means you're called upon to play a role. With practice, you'll get the hang of it.

LOVE AND RESPECT

One thing that it is important to understand is that disciplining your child won't make her love you any less. People who think discipline is the same as harsh punishment are getting the wrong end of the stick. Discipline means teaching your child how to behave and giving him boundaries and limits. It means praise and encouragement as much as firm and fair control.

Even in the most chaotic families I've visited, there's always been plenty of love around. But sometimes there hasn't been much respect. If a child doesn't respect her parents or her siblings, she's going to carry the same attitude into other situations—when she meets other children or when she starts at nursery or school—with potentially explosive results. In a good parent–child relationship, there's love and respect on both sides.

Talking to your child

You've had a bad morning. Your toddler has been up to all his usual tricks and is now running riot in the living room. "Stop it," you say. He pays no attention. "Stop it right now! NO! Don't touch that!" Your words fall on deaf ears. "Did you hear what I said? Stop it RIGHT NOW!"

Stop it! Stop it! Stop it! Don't touch! Don't touch! Don't touch! Shouting at your child in this kind of relentless way only communicates one thing: the fact that you're really wound up. If your child has been trying to get your attention by behaving naughtily, at this point he'll know he's succeeded.

Constantly shouting or screaming at your child is not going to change his behavior for the better. It's far more upsetting for both you and your child than disciplining him sensibly, and it raises the emotional temperature to boiling point. Who's lost control now?

Let's look at the other extreme. Say you pride yourself on not being the type of parent who loses their cool. You wouldn't ever dream of shouting or screaming. Instead you say something like: "Please don't do that. Oh, come on now, please don't do that." You smile.

And still nothing happens.

The first step in learning how to discipline your child is learning how to talk to her.

GO LARGE

When you're talking to children, they don't just focus on what you're saying. In fact, it might sail right over their heads if you use long words or make it too complicated. Instead, kids take in the whole package: your tone of voice, your body language, whether you're unsure, worried or anxious. They have powerful antennae. Sometimes I think they've got a sixth sense that we adults have forgotten all about.

Go large when you communicate with them. Exaggerate your expressions. It's a bit like role play. Many parents do this instinctively, but some don't because it makes them feel self-conscious or silly. Let your inhibitions go—be confident and playful when you talk to your child and when you respond to what he's saying. If you refer to yourself in the third person, it can take the heat out of the battle of wills sometimes. "Mom's going to wash your hands now."

THE VOICE OF AUTHORITY

When your child has done something wrong, you need to communicate that fact with the Voice of Authority:

★ Go to your child. Don't shout from halfway across the room.

★ Get down to her level so you don't intimidate her with your height. Crouch on your heels so you can make direct eye contact with her. You are not issuing commands from above that she can pretend to ignore.

★ Hold your child by the arms so she can't run away or interrupt eye contact. Say, "Look at me, please" if she tries to turn away.

★ Don't be threatening and don't grit your teeth!

★ Adopt a low, firm, authoritative tone. This is not an angry tone, a threatening tone, a belittling tone or a bargaining tone. It is a tone that leaves the child in no doubt that you mean business. It communicates displeasure.

★ Tell her clearly, calmly and sternly what she's done wrong: "Hitting people is not allowed. You don't hit other people. I don't want you to do it again, please."

Sometimes, miraculously, that will be all it takes. Small children are experts at picking up subtle signals. A low, firm voice and confident body language may be enough to get your message across.

What the Voice of Authority communicates is that there are limits or boundaries that the child must not cross. It also separates the bad behavior from the child herself. That's essential. It is the behavior that is bad and not the child—don't label her. The point is not to give her a tongue-lashing that makes her feel utterly worthless or to terrify her with a display of anger but to make it crystal clear that the behavior is wrong and that it does not please you.

Authority doesn't always come naturally to people. Some parents have to work a bit on their own confidence and self-belief in order to assert themselves in this way. If you are at all uncertain, your child will hear that in your voice. Practice in front of the mirror if necessary.

THE VOICE OF APPROVAL

When was the last time you praised your child? When was the last time you gave him unqualified approval? It's been half an hour and he hasn't gone after the cat or his little brother. He's eaten his lunch (most of it). He's allowed himself to be buckled into his car seat without a fuss. For a toddler, half an hour of trouble-free behavior is a long time. If you don't mark each of those small accomplishments with your approval, he'll think you haven't noticed.

He's been as good as gold and you haven't said a thing. What would it take to get your attention? How about chasing the cat? Tipping his bowl on the floor? Hitting his brother? When good behavior gets no attention, your child will try the one thing he knows that will work.

Don't be stingy with praise. Praising a child for good behavior will not make her big-headed or spoiled. And good behavior doesn't have to be anything big time. It can just be the absence of bad behavior. Many parents see that their kids are behaving well and think to themselves, "Phew. They aren't acting up at the moment. That gives me a chance to get on with other things." And off they go. What they forgot to do was communicate to their children that they noticed their good behavior and appreciated it.

One situation where praise is often overlooked is when one child is behaving well and the other is acting up. Good behavior can be almost invisible when a full-blown tornado is tearing through the living room trying to get your attention. You have to deal with the bad behavior, but you also mustn't forget to notice and praise the child who's quietly getting on with things.

Positive reinforcement is an essential part of discipline. You try to steer your child in the direction of the behavior you would like by praise and encouragement, and steer her away from the behavior you don't like by keeping the boundaries in place.

The Voice of Authority is low, firm and controlled. The Voice of Approval is the opposite. Many parents instinctively talk to their babies in a high voice. That's the same tone you should use for praise. A high-pitched, even excitable, tone communicates your pleasure. You can clap, whoop or cheer as well.

"Good boy! You ate your lunch!" Explain how this makes you feel. "Mommy's very pleased with you!"

Reassuring squeeze on the shoulder. "Look how beautifully you're playing!"

"Well done! You were a big help to Daddy."

THE VOICE OF REASON

Your toddler picks up lots of clues. She's got limited understanding in many ways. She can't reason like an adult, but she can read between the lines. Your tone of voice and body language will speak volumes to her. And, surprisingly, even in the case of small children, whose command of language may be pretty basic, the way you phrase things will also affect the way they respond.

You can save yourself a great deal of trouble by being careful about how you put things into words. Think before you speak. If you bargain, he will bargain. Don't plead with your child: ask and tell. You can't appeal to their better natures if you don't ask them properly. Always say "please." Common courtesy costs nothing.

I'm constantly amazed at how many choices parents offer their small children. A child of two and a half or three simply cannot choose between six, eight, ten options. Older kids, from around four or five upward, can begin to cope with simple choices and decisions.

Many parents hate the idea of telling a child what to do. They think that makes them dictators, not the loving parents they want to be. Instead of telling a child what to do, they offer choices in the hope that their kids will see them as kind and caring.

In other situations, choices are offered as a last-ditch attempt to head off a meltdown. Your child is resisting your attempts to get him dressed. You interpret this as meaning that he doesn't want to wear the blue trousers. So you start offering him choices to try to keep him happy. "Do you want to wear the green trousers instead? No? How about the red ones?" By the time you've gone through the entire wardrobe, you're back to square one and he's still wearing no trousers at all.

Not offering choices doesn't mean you should be abrupt, barking out commands left, right and center like a sergeant-major. You can still get the same message across if you ease your child along using a combination of clear directions, involvement and praise. "Let's put your socks on, please. You can pull up your socks. Well done. Now put your shoes on for Mommy."

Bargaining is just as bad as offering choices. Say your toddler won't eat her lunch:

★ You tell her that if she eats FIVE more spoonfuls, she can have a chocolate cookie.

★ She eats one more spoonful and asks for the cookie.

★ It seems to be working, but you haven't got all day. You tell her that if she eats THREE more spoonfuls she can have the cookie.

★ She says she wants the cookie now.

★ You can see where this is heading, but you don't want to give way. You tell her she can have the cookie when she eats just TWO more spoonfuls. You pick up the spoon and steer it toward her mouth. She bats the spoon away and starts really fussing for the cookie.

★ You tell her she can't have the cookie until she has ONE more spoonful.

★ She starts to scream with rage.

★ You give her the cookie.

★ She's won. She's had precisely one spoonful of lunch and one chocolate cookie. And now she wants another cookie.

Small children will always win contests like these because they don't really understand what a bargain or a promise is all about. What you're dangling in front of them in the form of a treat is just too tempting, and they will try their utmost to get it right now. And what you see as a trade-off, she sees as a rule that keeps changing—which, as everyone knows, is a rule that isn't really a rule at all and doesn't have to be followed.

HOW TO TALK TO YOUR CHILD:

* Don't scream and shout. Use the Voice of Authority for bad behavior.

* Praise your child when he's behaving well.

* Try to talk to your child in a positive way as much as possible. Instead of always telling him what you don't want him to do, try putting it in a different way. Instead of saying, "Don't put your dirty hands all over the sofa," say, "Let's wash your hands now. They're dirty. Then you can sit on the sofa and I'll read you a story."

* Don't be abrupt or bark out commands. You'll get instant resistance.

* Never use hurtful words or label your child. Make it clear it's the bad behavior you don't like, not your child.

* Be courteous.

* If your child shouts back at you, don't rise to the bait. A screaming match does no one any good. Tell your child not to speak to you in that manner.

* Don't compare your child unfavorably with his brothers and sisters, and never, ever talk about him to a third party within earshot. He might not look like he's listening, but he'll have caught every word.

* Don't offer too many choices to a small child.

* Don't bargain with her when she's having a tantrum.

* Go large. Let her read your body language. Be playful in the way you talk to your child.

Avoidance strategies

Avoidance strategies play an important role in controlling children's behavior. Very young children, who are just coming into toddlerhood, are at a stage when they are most impulsive and reckless. Involvement techniques and similar strategies work well at this age. If you can see it coming, and you can head it off, you'll save yourself unnecessary and exhausting conflicts.

★ Make sure your home is safe, secure and free of temptations. Why waste time and energy trying to keep precious objects out of a toddler's hands, when you could simply remove them from the scene altogether? See Action Stations, page 42.

★ Get to know which times of the day are most fractious and see if you can't improve matters by altering your routine. Bringing a mealtime forward by half an hour is much better than having to face half an hour of whining brought on by low blood sugar every day.

★ Work out which activities are causing the most upset. If your attempts to wash your child's hair lead to regular explosive outbursts at bathtime and wreck the bedtime routine, set aside another time in the day to get out the shampoo. It'll still be a problem, but some problems you can choose when to tackle.

★ Don't expect your child to wind down immediately after a period of boisterous play. She's not going to come indoors after chasing around the park and settle right down.

★ Don't rush a child from one activity to the next. Give him clear warnings at regular intervals about what's coming next so that he has time to prepare himself.

★ If there's a particular toy or game that always leads to a dispute, put it away for the time being. Don't let it become a bone of contention day after day.

★ Don't go looking for perfection or have unreasonably high expectations of your child's behavior. Know what to expect at each stage of the game.

★ If you can see trouble heading your way, try a distraction or diversion. Point out something interesting that's happening outside. "Do you see that little bird in the garden? What do you think he's doing?" Or invite your child to help you with a household chore. Take advantage of her short attention span to steer her away from trouble.

The involvement technique

The Involvement Technique is one of my favorites. It works really well with small children. The technique can be a big help when it comes to dealing with jealousy. It can even turn around that typical toddler flashpoint, supermarket shopping (see page 170).

Small children need attention. When they don't get it, they act up. The trouble is that there simply aren't enough hours in the day for you to give your toddler the attention he wants and deal with everything else as well. When you have two or more kids, short of cloning yourself, you have to think of ways around the problem.

You can't always expect a small child to play contentedly while you get on with sorting the laundry, washing the dishes or feeding his little brother. This might work once or twice if your child is in the right mood to get stuck into play. But chances are it won't work all the time, particularly if your child already resents the attention you're paying to a younger sibling.

The answer is to get the child involved with what you're doing. Small children don't find tasks like cleaning, sorting, fetching and carrying as boring as their older brothers and sisters sometimes do. Small children love to help. Helping makes them feel responsible and gives them confidence. They see it as a challenge they are succeeding in.

Of course, you have to give your child a job that suits what he can do, otherwise you'll just be adding to the long list of toddler frustrations, not to mention asking for mayhem and breakage. It's very important that you don't set him up for failure. But while you wouldn't expect him to be able to stack a dishwasher or run the vacuum cleaner over the living room carpet, there are plenty of ways he can join in. When you're changing a duvet cover, he can hold a corner for you. When you're washing the car, you can wrap him up in a raincoat and give him his own sponge and bucket of water. When you're washing vegetables, you can stand him beside you on a chair and let him wash a potato or two. Toy appliances are also a great idea. Little kids love mini dustpans and brushes. Chores may take a little bit longer and things might get a little messier, but you'll get the chore done and your child will get the benefit of your attention.

Most importantly, when you've got to attend to younger siblings, you can nip jealousy in the bud by involving your older child in the same activity. Asking her to fetch a toy or a washcloth at bathtime or to help spoonfeed the baby means you can pay her attention at the same time as you pay attention to her younger sibling. That way, you kill two birds with one stone.

The Involvement Technique allows you to keep paying attention to your child by talking about whatever you're doing at the time. And an important part of it is praise. Thank your child for her efforts, tell her what a good job she's doing and how it has helped you.

How to discipline your child

When your child does something really unacceptable—and you can see he's done it on purpose—or if he has settled into a pattern of naughty behavior, you have to take further steps and back up your rules with firm and fair control. The techniques outlined in the following sections are appropriate for children over the age of two and a half. Unless your child is very advanced for his age, that is the youngest you can start using these methods and expect results. Before then, a child's reasoning is not developed enough to understand what you're trying to teach him.

The main reason for bad behavior in kids between the ages of two and five is attention-seeking to get a reaction. The number two reason is jealousy, which, in a funny sort of way, amounts to the same thing. Small children will do almost anything to keep the spotlight trained on themselves. With the arrival of a new sibling, there's suddenly serious competition for your attention.

There are two important things to remember about using any method of discipline:

- Be consistent. Stick to your guns. Don't change the rules. Both parents must follow through the same way and back each other up. A child who's being disciplined by one parent will naturally go to the other to see if there's any mileage to be gained by that. Good cop, bad cop may work in television police dramas, but inconsistency in parenting makes disciplining impossible.

- Act immediately. Don't put off taking action. Toddlers don't remember things for very long. They won't associate the discipline with the bad behavior if there's too big a gap between the two.

WHEN NOT TO DISCIPLINE:

When a child is ill or recovering from illness. Some parents find that a sure sign of illness is when their boisterous toddler suddenly becomes much easier to deal with. Other children will have a shorter fuse when they're ill or teething. A sick child needs the right treatment and plenty of TLC.

When there is considerable doubt about who did what to whom. Most small children are pretty transparent, and you'll be able to tell who was the guilty party in a dispute that happened behind your back. But if a child gets repeatedly disciplined for things he hasn't done, he'll have every right to feel persecuted and will start to lie.

When the bad behavior has given her a real shock and she's genuinely sorry. She may have broken a vase she's been repeatedly warned not to touch, and the accident has shocked her into floods of tears. She's already learned the hard way, and chances are she won't do that again. (You've learned the hard way, too, for not putting the vase out of reach.) Accept the accident and talk to her about why it happened. Remind her of the rules and leave it at that. Discipline when a child is already upset and sorry for what she's done is giving her the wrong message.

When there's maximum disruption. Expect your child's behavior to go downhill if his world has been turned upside down by moving house, the birth of a new baby, family illness, or similar. Don't worry about discipline too much until the tension dies down. You have to make leeway for the emotional upset.

When he's already been disciplined. Don't discipline a child twice for the same offense. If he's been disciplined already by your partner or another caregiver, the incident is over.

The naughty step technique

The basic idea behind this technique is to remove the child from the scene for a few minutes and allow her time to cool down, think about what she's done and get ready to apologize. The point is to teach her that a particular type of unacceptable behavior will result in this consequence. This not only shows your child very clearly and effectively that she has crossed a line and broken an important rule, it also serves to take the tension out of the situation. You need that breathing space as much as she does.

The naughty step doesn't have to be a step. It can be a corner or a room. I like to use a step because it's away from the rest of the household, but not so far removed that you have to keep running up and down the stairs all the time. If you don't have stairs, you could put your child in the corner of the room, or even put her in another room altogether.

If you do use a room, use one that offers the child no distraction or stimulation. Putting your child in a roomful of toys or where there's a TV defeats the point of the exercise. She needs to be somewhere where she's going to be bored, where she's got time to think about things. In the first program of the American series of *Supernanny* I visited a family where the two children, aged six and two, were sent to their bedrooms when they behaved badly. The trouble with this arrangement is that it gave the children a mixed message. You want your child to feel comfortable and secure in his own bedroom, not to associate it with a place of discipline.

The Naughty Step Technique is the same as what many child care experts call "Time Out." Personally, I don't think it does children any harm to know that when they've been naughty, they have to sit on the "naughty" step. But if a different name makes it easier for you to use the technique, it really doesn't matter.

Your jealous four-year-old has pushed his little sister and thrown a toy at her. She's fallen over and has started to wail. It's all going awry. You'll be furious; you might be worried and panicky, too. Check first that your daughter is okay, resist the adrenaline surge that makes you want to yell at the top of your lungs, and put the Naughty Step Technique into practice.

HOW IT WORKS

This technique can break the cycle of bad behavior very quickly. But remember that you and your partner have to be consistent. And don't leave out a stage. The Warnings and the Explanations are essential. If in the heat of the moment you go straight to C, bypassing A and B, the method won't work.

THE WARNING Go to your son, come down to his level and look him straight in the eye. Use the Voice of Authority to give him a verbal warning. Say, "That behavior is unacceptable. We don't push people or throw things at them. It's wrong. Please don't do it again." The Warning is a key stage in the technique. It gives your child the chance to correct his own behavior. If you leave out the Warning, you've given him nowhere to go.

THE ULTIMATUM Five minutes later, your child does the same thing again. This time, using the same low, firm tone and confident body language, you issue an Ultimatum. Say, "I told you not to push your sister or throw things at her. That was very naughty. We don't push people. The next time you do it, you're going to the Naughty Step."

THE NAUGHTY STEP As soon as the bad behavior is repeated, take your child straight to the step. Sit him down and tell him to stay there. How long you should make him stay there will depend on his age. A couple of minutes is long enough for a two-and-a-half-year-old. Five minutes is about right for four-year-olds and over.

THE EXPLANATION Like the Warning, this is another key stage. Before you leave your child, explain why he's been put on the step. Say, "We don't push people or throw things at them. It's unacceptable behavior. People will get hurt. You're going to sit here for five minutes and think about what you've done. When five minutes is over, I will come and get you and I want you to apologize, please. Now stay there."

THE APOLOGY If he bounces off the step a few seconds later, march him back there and repeat the Explanation. Don't leave him for any longer than five minutes. At the end of that time, tell him you want him to apologize. But if he reappears before the five minutes is up and is genuinely sorry, let him stay. He must say what he's apologizing for. "Sorry" is a step in the right direction, but "Sorry for pushing my sister" is much better. People often ask me how you can tell whether an apology is genuine or not. I always say it's not the word, it's the manner in which it is delivered. I think it's fair to say that if a child has shouted "SORRY!" at the top of his lungs, it's not genuine.

PRAISE When he's apologized, praise him for it. This is important. You need to show your child that you have forgiven him for his bad behavior. "Thank you. That's more like it." Go back to your normal voice. He'll hear the difference in the higher tone.

IT'S OVER As soon as the child has apologized and you've praised him, treat the incident as closed. Invite him to play or to join in with whatever he was doing before. He's had the discipline, it's over, and now he must know he has a chance to make a fresh start.

The one-strike-and-you're-out technique

The Naughty Step Technique generally works wonders. In some cases, however, particularly if the child is older or the bad behavior is more ingrained, you may need to try something else.

When the Naughty Step Technique doesn't work, it may be because the child is still reveling in the attention she's getting, even if that attention is negative. One-Strike-And-You're-Out can break this pattern by showing her that bad behavior doesn't warrant any of your attention at all.

One important thing. Don't go straight to this technique. It won't work. Use the Naughty Step (or corner or room) first to establish that you're in charge. If you react to bad behavior by going straight to One-Strike-And-You're-Out, your child will feel that he's being ignored and will carry on behaving badly to get your attention.

On *Supernanny*, I visited a family where single mom Kelly was struggling to keep her two children, Sophie and Callum, under any form of control. The two kids showed no respect for their home, its contents, their toys, their mom, their grandma or each other. There was constant fighting, destruction and aggression. After we introduced the Naughty Corner and then Toy Confiscation, Callum's behavior improved in an incredibly short space of time. Five-year-old Sophie, however, continued to be very challenging, using aggressive behavior to prevent Kelly from spending any quality time with her little brother. Callum was being good as gold, but his efforts were going unnoticed while Sophie was lashing out, kicking and screaming. We had already done a lot of work on Kelly's voice control, but Sophie's screaming was really getting to her. What really made the difference was this crisis technique.

★ There's no verbal warning with this method. When the child behaves badly, remove her from the room. You don't have to take her to a special place, just exclude her from your presence. Tell her that her behavior is unacceptable and she can come back when she is ready to behave nicely and apologize.

★ If she comes back into the room to challenge you—as she will—remove her again. Don't pay her any attention. Say, "I'm not interested." Avoid eye contact.

★ Use voice control. Say, "Please leave the room" in a low, authoritative voice, so you don't have to physically remove her each time.

★ Keep it up until she says she is sorry. This will happen sooner than you think. Removing attention completely from a child who is used to getting it for bad behavior always comes as a complete shock. She's rung all your bells, and then some, and you haven't responded like you usually do. No wonder she's thrown.

★ When she has apologized, praise her and ask her to join in and play.

TOY CONFISCATION

Toy Confiscation is a disciplinary technique for older kids rather than toddlers. It's pointless for the younger age group, who can't really understand the bargaining that's involved. I think it's most useful if there's a problem that involves toys in the first place—if children are destructive, if they don't respect their belongings or if they are constantly fighting over them.

Don't devalue the technique by buying him a new toy for good behavior. That tells him immediately that no matter how many toys you confiscate, he's always going to be able to get more.

REWARDS

Positive attention and praise are the most effective rewards for children. They are immediate, and reinforce good behavior on the spot.

For an older child, you might like to use a star chart or stickers as well as praise. The star or the sticker is usually enough to back up her progress. If you want, you might like to give her a treat when she's gained a number of stars or stickers in a row—five, say, not twenty! This form of reward is often better if it comes out of the blue—but the surprise only works once. The next time you use a chart, she'll expect to be rewarded in the same way again. So be careful how you reward, or you might cause problems for yourself. Little treats are perfectly okay.

What you shouldn't do is go over the top and reward the child excessively for good behavior. If he's always getting a toy for doing what he should be doing anyway, he'll quickly catch on that he can manipulate his behavior to empty your wallet. He'll up the stakes while he's at it. One day and it's a sticker to eat his lunch. The next, it's Legos.

SMACKING

You'll have noticed that I have got all the way through an entire chapter on discipline without once mentioning smacking. I'm a nanny—smacking is not a form of discipline that nannies use, or should ever use, and rightly so. Whether you think it's all right to smack once in a while or completely unacceptable at any time, I'm not going to enter that debate.

All I will say is that the controversy that surrounds the whole issue puts some people off the idea of discipline altogether, and I think that's a pity. Children do need discipline, boundaries and limits. I hope this chapter has shown there are lots of effective ways you can put those boundaries in place and keep your sanity at the same time.

Dressing

Parents expect battles over clothing when their kids get older. The hip huggers! The miniskirts! The crop tops! Many are unprepared for problems earlier on, but I've seen families in which dressing a toddler and keeping that child dressed had turned into a day-long struggle. Like most other areas of conflict involving children, dressing was not always the real issue.

Sometimes dressing can be a challenge when a child wants more independence. He wants to dress himself, and he wants to choose what to wear. But if you are facing problems in a lot of different areas and he's refusing to dress, eat, wash, play nicely, and is generally behaving badly across the board, it's just another control issue.

Parents often deal with dressing problems by offering too many choices. Your three-year-old won't let you dress her in trousers. You think maybe that means she wants to wear a dress. No? Well then, maybe she doesn't like that particular dress. You try another dress. And another. You go back to the trousers. By now she's running down the stairs wearing nothing at all.

Whether or not your toddler has an opinion about what she would like to wear, if you react to a refusal to get dressed by offering too many choices, each choice you offer is simply a sign to your child that you've given in and she's winning the battle. What she really wants may have nothing to do with clothes at all: her desire is simply to get her own way. Another way parents often respond to this kind of situation is by trying to dress their child as if he were still a baby who couldn't even put his own arm into a sleeve. If you try to force a child to get dressed, you'll soon come up against a physical limit—yours. Toddlers aren't helpless babies. They can kick, wriggle, squirm, run off—and they will. To cap it all, they'll have a tantrum. And all you wanted to do was put his shoes on.

Dressing often becomes an issue because it's rushed. To a parent, dressing or undressing their child is something that has to be done—quickly, quickly!—before something else can happen—going on an outing, picking older children up from school, getting ready for bed. You've got your eye on the clock. You want to hurry things along. However, at the slightest hint that she's being rushed, your toddler will dig in her heels. That's how getting your child dressed can end up taking all day.

This kind of problem can be turned around very quickly using a combination of techniques. The first is to be clear about what you would like your child to wear, and to cut down on the choices you put in front of him. The second is to involve him in what you're doing and encourage him to learn to dress himself. And the third is to back up repeated struggles with firm and fair control.

What are we going to wear today?

"What are we going to wear today?" is not a question you should be asking a young child. If you ask that question, you might think to yourself that you're being kind by inviting your child to have a say in what he wears, or that you're sidestepping a potential explosion by getting him to choose. Your toddler will immediately think that a) you don't know the answer—otherwise why are you asking him?—and b) dressing is optional. All that choices offer young children is uncertainty. Someone has to be in charge: that means it's up to him to take over. And he will.

If you offer full choice to an older child who's more capable of having an opinion on what she would like to wear but still doesn't know how to make choices appropriately, don't be surprised if she picks a spangly summer top for an outing to the park in midwinter. It's only fair to offer an older child some say in what she wears. But instead of allowing her to pick anything from her wardrobe, offer her a choice between two or three things, all of which are suitable for the occasion and the weather. Or you can sidestep the problem by putting summer clothes away in the winter and vice versa, just like you might rotate your own wardrobe.

Do listen to a child if she repeatedly refuses to wear a particular item of clothing on the grounds of discomfort. Pay attention to her if she says a top is too tight every time she wears it. Some children hate the feeling of wool next to the skin and say it feels too "itchy." Too bad if the jumper was lovingly handknitted by your aunt— if it feels like a hairshirt to your child, don't make her wear it.

One way you can take the heat out of dressing disputes and also relieve some of the time pressure is to lay clothes out the night before. Pick out the clothes and explain to your child that he's going to be wearing those jeans and that top tomorrow, and then you'll be going round to his friend's house. Then getting dressed isn't an issue in itself, it's part of something to look forward to, which includes an outing.

Encouraging your child to dress

If you think about it from a child's point of view, being dressed by someone else must be a bit alarming at times. One second your arms are shoved down sleeves, then your legs are forced into tights and before you know it, a skirt comes down over your head and you can't see or breathe properly.

If you dress a child in a hurry, chances are you won't be as gentle as you should be, or take the time to prepare her for what's coming next. You wouldn't like it if someone more than twice your size threw a jersey over your head without warning, or yanked your arms to force them down sleeves, or zipped up in such a hurry that it pinched your skin.

Even when a child is quite young, you can start encouraging her to dress herself. The first stage is to involve her in the process so she doesn't feel rushed from pillar to post. Keep talking and telling her what you're doing and what you're going to do next.

"Now let's put on your top. Can you put your arm in the sleeve, please? Well done. Now you try the other arm." Lots of praise makes it go smoothly.

The second stage is to encourage more active involvement. Make it easy for your child to learn to dress himself by choosing clothes that don't have complicated fastenings. He's not going to be able to tie his own shoelaces or do up fiddly buttons, but he can pull up a zip or tug at a strap. Shoes that fasten with Velcro are better for young children than those with laces or buckles.

Play is another way of encouraging a child to dress herself. What else is dressing and undressing dolls all about? Or you might buy her one of those educational toys designed to help teach children basic dressing skills such as doing up buttons or tying shoelaces.

While she's learning how to dress, things are still going to be frustrating, and frustration can turn into a tantrum in the blink of an eye. Don't set her up for failure. Don't just decide one day that she's perfectly capable of doing it herself, then leave her to it and stand back ready to correct her when she gets it wrong. Show her and involve her. Put on one of her shoes, then ask her to put on the other one. Explain how to do it. "Put the strap through the buckle—that's it! Now pull it through."

PROBLEM:
REFUSING TO GET DRESSED/ UNDRESSED

Small children often prolong or avoid dressing as a way of delaying bedtime. It's not the clothes that are the issue. Having exactly the right pair of pants with exactly the right label in exactly the right color won't be a problem until later. And, although many toddlers love to remove all or part of their clothes and run around stark naked, they aren't particularly anti-clothes as such. They're just delighting in a new skill—the undoing (or undressing) always comes before the doing.

Children who turn dressing and undressing into repeated episodes of screaming and kicking need firm and fair control. It might seem like a petty issue, but if you don't tackle it, you're heading off down the path where dressing can turn into a day-long struggle.

SOLUTION:
AVOIDANCE/THE NAUGHTY STEP TECHNIQUE

★ Allow plenty of time in your daily routine for getting your child dressed. You can throw on your clothes in seconds, and might barely consider dressing an activity at all, but your child needs much longer.

★ Lay out clothes the night before and don't offer a toddler too much choice over what he wears. Two choices are enough for a toddler. He hasn't the sense to make a choice on grounds of suitability, and style is completely irrelevant to him. Left to his own devices, he might be happy going to the supermarket in the nude or wearing his pants on his head.

★ For a three-year-old child, you can increase the choices to three outfits that are suitable for the occasion and the weather.

★ Involve your child and encourage her to dress herself by giving her small achievable tasks.

★ Keep up a running commentary that is positive and involving. Give plenty of praise. Make it fun—even make it silly.

★ If dressing becomes a real issue—if it leads to defiance, aggression and other forms of bad behavior—use the Naughty Step Technique (see page 80). Remember to include the Warning and Explanation.

PROBLEM:
THE FAD DRESSER

It doesn't have to be Halloween for you to see a fair number of fairy princesses or action heroes doing the shopping with their parents on Saturday morning. In fact, I've walked Spiderman down the street before. If your child is reasonably cooperative about getting dressed most of the time and hasn't turned the whole issue into a battle of wills, it does her no harm at all to wear the fairy dress to the supermarket or put on the tights that make an eye-watering clash with the skirt. Parents need to learn to chill out. Fancy dressers aren't always fad dressers.
Let kids be kids and dress up. It's part of their play.

When it does start to matter is when your child develops a fad for a particular color or piece of clothing that means he won't wear anything else but green, or the T-shirt with the dinosaur on the front. If you give in to this, it can go on for months.

SOLUTION:
AVOIDANCE

★ Be on the lookout for signs of fad dressing. It's far easier to nip this in the bud than it is to get the child out of a pattern of behavior that has been going on for ages.

★ You may need to go back a step if your child shows signs of fad dressing. Instead of offering limited choice, offer none at all. Lay out the clothes the night before and remove the outfit that she is becoming obsessed with. Tell her that it's in the wash—it'll need it by now!

★ Give plenty of positive reinforcement for those occasions when she gets dressed without turning it into a huge exercise. A star chart can be a good way of showing your approval.

Washing

Washing—bathing, brushing the teeth, washing and detangling the hair, washing hands and face, cutting fingernails and toenails—are activities that are closely associated with dressing and undressing in the daily routine. Most small children enjoy water and don't need too much encouragement to make a splash in the sink or the bath.

What they will need, as well as plenty of hands-on help and supervision, are constant reminders to follow through with the routine. A toddler won't skip brushing his teeth or washing his hands because he hates the idea of clean teeth or clean hands—it'll just have gone straight out of his head.

🦆 Give clear, repeated warnings leading up to any change of activity, especially if your child is in the middle of doing something else, like finishing a jigsaw puzzle. Think about it from their point of view. You wouldn't like it if you were in the middle of sending an e-mail and someone told you to stop and take out the rubbish. Kids often refuse to get in the bath when bathtime has been sprung on them out of the blue. It's not that they don't like having a bath—in fact, they'll be perfectly happy in the bath once you've got them there—it's just that they don't like stopping one thing and starting another with no warning. You'll have the same sort of refusal when it's time to get out of the bath if you don't prepare them in the same way.

🦆 Don't ask, tell. "I want you to brush your teeth now, please" or "Teeth please!" is a better reminder than a question, which always invites "No" or "I don't want to."

🦆 Use the Involvement Technique when you need to split your attention between your toddler and his younger siblings. Get him to help you with simple tasks, like putting toothpaste on a brush, and give him plenty of praise for it.

🦆 Let your child see you brush your teeth, wash your hair and wash your face. Children pick up a lot from watching you, even more than they pick up from listening to you. They also learn from watching older children. Explain what you're doing—"Let's get all those potatoes and carrots off your teeth"—but show them at the same time. "I'm going to do my teeth, too."

🦆 I like to use mime and singsong. "This-is-the-way-we-brush-our-teeth (or wash our face), brush-our-teeth, brush-our-teeth…"

🦆 A pea-sized amount of toothpaste is enough, as there's fluoride in the water, too. Encourage young children to brush their own teeth, but brush the teeth again after they've finished so you make sure the back teeth are cleaned.

🦆 Some kids hate having their hair washed. It might be the water that scares them, the fear of water going up their nose, shampoo stinging their eyes, or it might be the shower nozzle that puts them off. Let your child watch you wash your own hair and explain what the shampoo and conditioner are for. Give her a washcloth to put over her face if that makes her feel more secure. You can also buy a hair shield that stops water and shampoo from running down her face. If she hates the shower nozzle, use a plastic cup to rinse her hair instead. I like to let children know when I'm about to rinse their hair. "One, two, three. On 'three,' JoJo's going to pour the water."

🦆 Always put a rubber mat down in the bath so a child can't slip. Test the water to make sure it's not too hot or cold—children scald very easily. Use a booster stool so she can reach the sink for teeth-brushing and face-washing. Children learn best when they can see what they're doing—they need to be able to look in the mirror.

Some children are reluctant to get in the bath at all. Take that seriously and don't force the issue. Try to find out what's behind it. It could just be that you're trying to bathe too many kids at the same time. If your child develops a real fear of water, build up his confidence gradually. Stand him in a baby bath and sponge him. Then move up to a bath in the baby bath with just a few inches of water before encouraging him to try the tub again. Go swimming with him to increase his confidence. Put him in the bath with you and show him that there's nothing to fear.

Make bathtime fun with toys and games. Bubble baths are exciting. You can also let your child blow bubbles in the bath—it's the perfect place for that kind of messy play. Play games of pretend—"Show me how you can be a dolphin!"

MY TOP TEN RULES

TO SUM UP, HERE'S HOW MY TOP TEN RULES APPLY TO DRESSING AND WASHING:

1. PRAISE AND REWARDS

Praise your child when he does something properly—it doesn't have to be the first time! Use a star chart to reinforce good behavior or to break the cycle of fad dressing.

2. CONSISTENCY

Make sure you and your partner follow the routine the same way and stick by the same rules. The same applies when you are encouraging your child to dress herself—don't undermine her attempts to learn by doing everything for her.

3. ROUTINE

Build enough time into your routine for dressing, especially at the beginning of the day. Don't expect it to take a matter of seconds.

4. BOUNDARIES

Don't offer small children too many choices about what to wear. Make it clear that you expect them to get dressed without fussing, and that you expect them to get dressed when they're told. At the same time, be realistic about what they can do and how fast they can do it.

5. DISCIPLINE

Back up your rules with firm and fair control. If dressing leads to aggression, defiance and other forms of unacceptable behavior, use the Naughty Step Technique and remember to include the Warning and Explanation.

6. WARNINGS

Remind your kids repeatedly when it's time to get dressed or washed, or when it's time get in or out of the bath. Don't spring sudden changes of activity on them. Let them know what's happening next.

7. EXPLANATIONS

Show and tell your child how to dress and wash and brush her teeth. Explain why it's important to be clean and what the different products are for. Keep up a running commentary in a fun way.

8. RESTRAINT

Don't shout and bark out commands to your child. Use a calm, authoritative voice. Don't rush your child or let her know that you are pressed for time. Don't try to force her into her clothes.

9. RESPONSIBILITY

Encourage your child to dress himself. Make it easy for him to learn by making sure his clothes don't have complicated fastenings. Use the Involvement Technique when you need to occupy yourself with your other kids.

10. RELAXATION

Make bathtime fun with games of "let's pretend." It's a good chance to unwind, relax and be silly before calming down for the night. The same kind of playful approach also works well with dressing.

Toilet training

A lot of parents are obsessed with getting their child out of diapers. Let me say that any child who is toilet-trained by two years old is doing incredibly well—and that's not meant to sound like a target you should be aiming for. Toilet training is far more likely to happen sometime between two and a half and three, at which time it will happen much more quickly. If you get the timing right, you can toilet-train your child in a week or two. If you start to train her before she is ready, or if you stop and start the training according to when it's convenient for you, expect it to go on for ages—even months.

Of course, getting a child out of diapers is a welcome stage for parents. But bear in mind that these days, with disposable diapers, you aren't saying good-bye to hours of laundering and soaking stinking terrycloth in pails of disinfectant and bleach, you're just crossing another item off your weekly shopping and removing a rather messy, smelly chore from your routine.

Although you shouldn't start training too early, what you can do is prepare your child for this stage when it does come by being relaxed and comfortable about natural bodily functions. I think we're far too uptight about these kinds of things. Toilet humor is a sure sign that many people still feel uncomfortable about what should be a simple fact of life—what goes in eventually comes out.

How to spot when your child is ready

The physical development that will eventually allow your child to control her bladder and her bowels happens at around 18 months. But it takes longer, usually another year or so, before she can recognize when she needs to go and can do something about it herself.

A baby will soil or wet himself as a reflex action, usually straight after eating and sometimes during it. Some time after the age of two, he will begin to notice before he goes that something's about to happen. He may announce the fact to you a few seconds in advance or even during a pee or poo. That on its own is not enough to bring out the underpants and the potty but it's a sign you're heading in the right direction.

Another way of telling whether the right time is approaching is to examine your child's diapers. Compare how much fluid she's taking in with how wet her diaper is when you put her down for her nap. If the diaper stays dry and clean for longer, she's getting to the point where voluntary control is not far off.

In most children, bowel control comes before bladder control—simply because there's slightly less urgency attached to the need to poo and so it's easier to hold on for a bit—although in others it can be the other way round. Being dry at night is always the last stage. When your child is really ready, you can toilet-train him so he is both clean and dry during the day, although don't expect to do without a diaper at night for some while yet.

Another reason why I think toilet-training too early is bound to fail is that communication is vital for success. At two, most children's command of speech will be sketchy at best. You need to be able to talk to her about the process and teach her how to spot the signs. She needs to be able to tell you—or anyone else who's looking after her—when she's ready to go. Parents can often spot from the look or posture of their toddler when they're getting ready to fill their diaper. But squatting or a predictable facial expression isn't enough to go on for toilet training.

If your child seems to be ready but there is disruption in the household—if you're moving, expecting a new baby, or any other out-of-the-ordinary event is just about to take place—put off the training until the disruption is over.

How to toilet-train

Prepare your child for training by taking any hint of shame or disgust out of what is simply a natural fact of life. Don't disappear behind a closed door when you go to the toilet. Keep the door open. Bring her into the toilet with you. Explain what's happening, what the toilet paper is for and show her how you wash your hands afterwards. If you prepare her in the right way, you can teach two things at once: toilet training and hygiene.

Equip yourself with a potty and a travel potty. I think potties should be kept plain and simple. Don't make them a big deal. They're not thrones, toys or seats, they're just accessible, portable toilets.

In the same way, I'm not a fan of pull-ups, which some people use as a halfway stage between diapers and underpants. It's either diapers or pants as far as I'm concerned. Anything else only confuses the issue. The only situation in which I would use pull-ups is where a child has learned how to take off his diaper at night.

While potties should be simple and plain, you can go to town with underpants. Here's an obvious reward for successful toilet training. Kids are usually thrilled to bits when they move into underpants. Motif underpants featuring favorite film or cartoon characters are even more exciting.

When toilet training coincides with warm weather, you can let your child run around bare-bottomed, provided you encourage her to keep using the potty. But that can sometimes be counter-productive. If a child doesn't learn what it feels like to be wet, she'll have less incentive for control. If she wets her pants, don't rush her out of them straight away. Let her learn that it's uncomfortable and it's something she should try to avoid.

TRAINING TIPS:

★ Learn to spot the signs when he needs to go. Clutching his crotch is an obvious one.

★ During the toilet-training period, keep clothing uncomplicated. Trousers with elasticated waists that can be pulled down quickly are better than dungarees with buttons, straps or zips.

★ Make a mental note of how much fluid you give your child throughout the day.

★ Explain what it feels like to want to go. "Do you feel it in your tummy?" Press your belly low down and show her what you're talking about. You don't have to go into graphic detail. It's not an anatomy lesson. Just try to get her to understand the connection between the feeling and what happens next.

★ When he's done a pee or a poo, praise him. Toilet training is entirely based around praise and approval. It requires constant positive reinforcement.

★ "Do you need to do pee pee?" Repeat yourself over and over and over. A million times a day if necessary.

★ Keep the potty close at hand, but don't put it in front of the TV. If it stays in front of the TV, it becomes a seat, and your child will lose his concentration and the message. Once he's starting to get the hang of it, keep the potty in the bathroom where it belongs.

★ Encourage your child by going to the toilet together.

★ Bear in mind that some kids are shy and like to go into a corner to use the potty. If your child wants privacy, give it to her.

★ As soon as toilet training starts, expose your child to different situations. Don't become housebound for the week or two weeks that it takes. Let him experience what it's like to go out into the cold. Go on outings to the park. Take him for a drive in the car. Don't put a diaper on him for these excursions. Take the travel potty and be prepared for a quick roadside stop. Keep it short and sweet.

★ Before you go out, take the initiative and tell your child to pee.

★ Be consistent. This is absolutely key. Your inconvenience is secondary. If you are going to your parents' house for the weekend, don't put your child back in diapers to avoid the hassle. If underpants are okay one minute and diapers are okay the next, she won't get the message.

★ Be calm and confident. Don't overload the situation with anxiety or blame, or try to rush things.

★ Don't be intrusive. When I sit a child on a toilet in a public place and have to steady her by holding on to her hands or her knees, I always look away so she can concentrate.

USING THE TOILET

A potty is a more secure place for a child to learn toilet training than the toilet, where she will be sitting with her feet swinging well above the floor and perched on a seat that is much bigger and wider than her bottom. Many young children find a flushing toilet pretty scary—especially if they're sitting on it!

At some stage, however, your child will be ready to leave her potty behind. Make it easy for her to adapt to using the toilet by giving her a step or stool so she can get onto it easily. Fit the toilet with a child seat so she won't feel as if she's going to fall through.

Take every opportunity to bracket toilet training with hygiene. Remind your child to wash his hands afterwards and see that he does. By the age of four or five, I think it's perfectly reasonable to expect a child to wipe his own bottom. Give him wet wipes if that makes it easier. You can always check after he's finished that he's done it properly.

ACCIDENTS

All kids have accidents, wet their pants and even soil themselves once or twice. These kinds of accidents often happen when a child has become overexcited or too distracted to pick up on what his body is trying to tell him. When that happens, your child will be upset. Don't make a big deal out of it. Excessive attention or comfort might eventually give a toddler the idea that accidents can have their uses. Simply treat the episode in a calm, matter-of-fact way. Tell him that these things happen, and forget about it.

You can help prevent accidents by having reasonable expectations. When a child says he wants to go, he wants to go. Take him seriously and don't expect him to be able to wait for very long.

Sometimes a child will have an accident because she's too lazy to take herself to the toilet or because she thinks she's going to miss out on something that's much more interesting. Let her know that this is not acceptable. If she's using an accident as a stalling tactic—holding on until it's at its most inconvenient—take that burden away from her. Take the initiative and suggest she goes to the toilet now. Before you get in the car.

Bedwetting is often a sign that you've left off the night-time diapers too soon. You need to see several dry ones in a row before you can leave off a diaper at night. But bedwetting can also indicate some kind of emotional upset. A strange bed is enough to set some kids off. It stands to reason that the arrival of a new baby brother or sister, a move or a bad nightmare may also lead to the same result. These are emotional issues and need to be addressed delicately and with no blame attached. Bedwetting also goes along with periods of illness.

If bedwetting is associated with a fear of the dark and the child's reluctance to make the trip to the toilet in the middle of the night, keep the potty in the bedroom at nighttime and add a night-light.

PROBLEM:
PERSISTENT BEDWETTING

Persistent bedwetting in an older child is far from rare. It's upsetting for the child, and it makes work for you. There are many reasons why this might be happening. Stress and emotional problems are often to blame. Sometimes a child may have developed a urinary infection. If you've ruled out the obvious causes and the accidents keep happening with depressing regularity, it may well be the case that she is using them as a means of getting attention.

If your child regularly wets the bed at night, don't be tempted to bring her into your own bed. Obviously, you don't want to discipline a child for bedwetting. But you shouldn't reward her, either.

SOLUTION:
BREAK THE PATTERN

Whatever the reason behind the bedwetting, the important thing is to break the pattern. The most effective way is to lift your child out of bed, sit him on the potty or the toilet and try to get him to pee last thing at night just before you go to bed. If he's normally a good sleeper, you can usually do this with a minimum of fuss, and he will fall straight back to sleep. It also makes sense to limit his fluid intake after supper. A child who drains a huge glass of milk or juice just before going to bed will find it harder to stay dry.

PROBLEM:
SOILING

This is a tricky one. Soiling often coincides with illness, times when your child is preoccupied, scared or distracted, or periods of family disruption. Always give your child the benefit of the doubt and keep on with the training. If you rush in and discipline for soiling, you can set the clock back on toilet training by months.

Some kids find bowel control much harder than bladder control. Others find bowel movements a real cause of anxiety. They may be scared of the motion itself or of seeing the result. For that reason, they try and hold on until nature takes over and they have a distressing accident. It's important to be sensitive, but don't over-pacify them. Say, "That's because you held it" in a light tone. "Never mind." Explain why they had the accident. One episode like this is usually upsetting enough to change things.

SOLUTION:
KEEP IT LOW-KEY

If accidents keep on happening, allow enough time in your routine for changing him out of his clothes and pack fresh underpants, wet wipes and clean trousers as a matter of course. Don't rush him on the potty. Don't give him the first idea that time is ticking past or that you are anxious about that fact. Each time he has an accident, clean him up but don't give him extra attention. As soon as he stops soiling himself, give him lots of praise.

Sometimes anxiety over bowel movements can lead to constipation. I always put children who are constipated for whatever reason into a warm bath. That helps the muscles to relax. If constipation is a regular problem, make sure there's enough fresh fruit and vegetables in the diet and your child is getting plenty of fluids.

MY TOP TEN RULES

**TO SUM UP, HERE'S HOW MY TOP TEN RULES
APPLY TO TOILET TRAINING:**

1. PRAISE AND REWARDS

Give plenty of praise and encouragement every step of the way.
Motif underpants are a great incentive.

2. CONSISTENCY

Once you start toilet training, don't stop for any reason. Keep it up,
even if it's going to cause you inconvenience. Don't use pull-ups as
a halfway stage—it confuses the issue.

3. ROUTINE

Don't rush things. Allow time for kids to go to the toilet before you
go out and remind them at every opportunity.

4. BOUNDARIES

Have realistic expectations of toilet training. Don't be tempted to start
too early or the whole process will drag on for months. Learn to spot
the signs of readiness. Keep potties in the bathroom where they
belong. Don't leave off the nighttime diaper too soon.

5. DISCIPLINE

Positive reinforcement is the key to toilet training. Never discipline
a child for accidents. Limit the chances of bedwetting by putting your
child on the potty or the toilet last thing at night before you go to bed.

6. WARNINGS

During the toilet-training period, keep asking your child over and over again if she needs to go to the toilet. Even after she's trained, keep asking her at key times of the day. Small children can't wait very long when they need to go.

7. EXPLANATIONS

Teach your child what it feels like to need to go. Show and tell her what happens in the bathroom—let her watch you go to the toilet and wash your hands afterward. Take the opportunity to teach her about hygiene.

8. RESTRAINT

Don't make a big deal of accidents or occasional bedwetting. Allow children their privacy if they ask for it.

9. RESPONSIBILITY

Encourage your child to wash her hands and wipe herself correctly as soon as she is able.

10. RELAXATION

Approach toilet training in an open and relaxed way. It's a natural part of life.

Eating

Feeding your child should be simple. There's no shortage of advice available on what makes a good balanced diet, and these days we don't have to hunt, gather or grow our food, we just have to go to the shops. You ought to be able to put a bowl or plate of nourishing food down in front of your child at breakfast, lunch and dinner and let hunger do the rest. If only it was that simple.

All too often mealtimes are battles fought on a number of fronts. First, there's that good nourishing food you've bought, prepared and cooked, but your child has decided tastes like poison. Then, there's the whole sitting-at-table issue, which has somehow become an optional extra as far as she is concerned. And, last but not least, there's what your child would *really* like to eat: snacks, chips, chocolate, sweets and sugary drinks. You've lost track of the number of times in the day when your child has demanded a cookie, but you certainly haven't heard her screaming for broccoli.

Like many other areas of daily life, eating is an activity where young children very soon start exercising their desire for independence. It doesn't take long for them to work out the obvious: *you can't make them eat.* Soon after they've worked that one out, they pick up on the fact that food is one of the things that their parents worry about the most.

It's understandable that parents worry about feeding their kids. From that first hungry newborn cry, you'll know that getting food into your child at regular intervals is vital for his development and growth. And you won't just know it, you'll feel it.

In the early weeks and months, feeding is a time of special closeness. It's often when the emotional bonds between parent and child are deepened and strengthened. Later on, if your child acts up at mealtimes or rejects the food you have given her, you're bound to find it difficult to be patient and objective. Feeding children is an emotional issue right from the start.

By setting routines, rules and boundaries, you can begin to take the emotional heat out of the situation so that mealtimes become something to enjoy again. When children are small and for some long while after, it's up to you to show them how to eat, just as much as it's your job to put the right sort of food in front of them. After all, no parent ever handed their child a cookie by accident!

Give your children a proper nutritional diet right from the start. Make it a way of life. Children aren't born craving sugar. If they're only given good, nutritional food, they won't know any different—a chopped-up peach will be as much of a treat for them as a bowl of ice cream might be for another child.

Feeding babies

Whether you're breastfeeding or bottle-feeding, all your baby needs in the first months of life is milk, with the optional addition of cooled boiled water. No solid foods at all should be introduced before four months; if he's hungry, he needs more milk, not his first taste of baby food. Introducing solid food before a child's stomach can digest it properly can result in problems. It can also lead to allergic reactions.

Breast milk is designed by nature to give a baby exactly what she needs: the right amount of fat, carbohydrate and protein, along with vitamins, minerals and important antibodies that boost her immune system at a time when otherwise she would be most vulnerable to infection. Although they won't deliver the same antibodies, modern baby-milk formulas have been specifically designed to be as close to breast milk as possible. Cow's milk is for calves; in the first year of life babies should not be given cow's milk even in diluted form because it contains far too much protein.

Breastfeeding

Even a few weeks of breastfeeding will help to give a baby a good start. But if you do decide to bottle-feed or find you have to give up breastfeeding for whatever reason, don't be hard on yourself or let other mothers make you feel inadequate. Your child will still be getting everything he needs.

Breastfeeding doesn't always come naturally. Many new mothers are not given enough help or instruction on feeding. Some find that they manage all right at the beginning, but run into problems further on. Such problems often occur when the baby does not latch on to the breast properly or when the supply of milk is out of step with what the baby requires.

Getting enough sleep and eating a healthy diet is ABSOLUTELY essential for moms. Stress can also have an impact on how much milk you produce.

LATCHING ON

A newborn baby will instinctively turn in the direction of a gentle stroke on one cheek—which feels the same as the soft touch of a breast. Presented with a nipple on that side, she will then begin to suck vigorously. When a baby is properly latched on, most of the brown area of the nipple—the aureole—is in her mouth, not just the nipple itself. If she only sucks from the end of the nipple, she will not drain the breast efficiently and in time you may end up with sore, cracked nipples and a buildup of milk in the milk ducts, which in turn can lead to the more serious problem of mastitis.

SUPPLY AND DEMAND

In the first two days, you won't produce milk at all. What you will produce is a thin watery fluid called colostrum, which contains important antibodies to protect your baby from infection. Two to three days after the birth, your milk will come in, sometimes accompanied by the tearfulness known as "three-day" or "baby" blues. After that, your breasts will produce milk in response to your baby's demands. Nature has arranged things so that the more times a baby sucks and feeds, the more milk you will produce.

A baby's growth may look like a smooth line on a chart, but it proceeds in a series of small jumps. You may well find that after a couple of weeks of predictable feeding, one day your baby suddenly seems to want to feed all the time. This is his way of boosting your milk supply to meet his growing needs. When he has succeeded in doing so, a pattern will return. At the same time, if your baby still seems to want more after a full feeding, it might be the case that he is trying to suck himself to sleep.

You can only meet your baby's need for milk if you are eating a proper diet, drinking plenty of fluids and getting enough rest yourself. The hunger and thirst that come with breastfeeding are intense. Some mothers like to keep a thermos of cocoa or hot soup by their bed so they can satisfy those pangs straightaway.

A lot of anxiety that surrounds breastfeeding has to do with the fact that you can't see how much your baby is getting. Most of the time that anxiety is misplaced. Regular trips to the doctor to have your baby weighed should put your worries to rest.

Bottle-feeding

Just as with breastfeeding, there's a technique to bottle-feeding. In this case, you need to ensure that your baby takes in milk at the right rate and without also taking in a lot of air that will make her uncomfortable. The hole in the nipple should be big enough so that several drops of milk flow through per second and the nipple itself should be big enough so that the baby can latch on properly. You can encourage her to do this by gently stroking her on one cheek to provoke the sucking response. She will then turn her head in the direction of the stroke, which is where the nipple should be. The bottle should be held at an angle so that the air pocket does not reach the nipple and cause gas. If a baby takes in too much air, burping may bring up the whole feeding. I always burp a baby halfway through a feeding as a matter of course.

Although on the face of it bottle-feeding ought to make it easy to see how much your baby's getting, it is still possible to underfeed. Make up a little extra milk per feeding than the recommended allowance in case he's hungrier than usual. If he drains the bottle, he might still need more. What you mustn't do, however, is increase the recommended ratio of formula to water. He won't get more food that way, just milk that is too concentrated for his system and this may make him constipated. It can also be a good idea to give your baby a drink of cooled boiled water from time to time, especially in hot weather, or if he's ill.

Bottle-feeding does have one great advantage. It enables you to share the feedings more easily with your partner. Make sure that you do.

Introducing solid food

Four to five months is the right sort of time to start your baby on solid food. You'll know it's the right time if he is demanding more and more meals, or if his weight gain has slowed for no reason. Don't expect an overnight switch from milk to solid food: at the beginning, you're just offering tastes to get him used to the idea. He'll still be getting most of his food intake from milk.

There's nothing like the expression that crosses a baby's face the first time she tastes her first solid food. It's not just the taste, it's the texture and consistency that come as such a surprise. She may take to it at once or she may not like it at all. Spitting out a mouthful of food doesn't necessarily mean she doesn't like it; it just means she doesn't know what to do with it yet. But if she shows a lot of resistance, wait a week or so and then try her on something else.

Foods should be introduced gradually. One at a time is best. That way you can see if any food is particularly disliked or if it causes a bad reaction. Begin by offering fairly bland, semisolid food such as baby rice or baby cereal mixed with breast milk or formula, or cooled boiled water. Pureed fruit and vegetables such as cooked carrot, potato, apple and pear, along with mashed-up banana and avocado, are also good early foods.

NEW TASTES:

★ Introduce solid food at a specific set time. It can be breakfast or lunch.

★ Use a plastic spoon to feed your baby and give him a spoon to hold, too. He won't be able to use it yet, but it may help to make the experience more fun for him.

★ At the beginning don't expect him to manage more than a couple of spoonfuls at a time once a day. At the beginning more of it will be on his bib or on the floor than in his mouth. He'll take time to get used to the idea. He isn't really spitting out the food, what he's doing is exploring it by pushing his tongue in and out of his mouth. That tends to make the food watery.

★ Be extra careful with hygiene.

★ If he turns his head away, either he's had enough or he doesn't like it. Don't force him to eat. Watch out for facial expressions.

★ Always test the temperature of the food to make sure it isn't too hot. You can buy spoons these days that indicate when food is too hot by turning a different color.

★ Mince, puree, grate, mash or strain food so there are no hard lumps that could cause choking.

★ At any signs of allergic reaction, do not hesitate to take your child immediately to the hospital.

WHAT TO AVOID

Introduce vegetables and fruit first, protein second. Separating the food groups allows you to keep an eye out for any allergic reactions. You should delay giving a baby certain types of food for longer. Allergies can result if a baby is introduced to food such as nuts, cow's milk and eggs too early. Signs to look out for include patches of reddened itching skin and sudden bouts of diarrhea or vomiting.

Watch out for these foods:

SALT Don't add salt to food or offer salty foods. This puts a strain on a young child's kidneys.

SUGAR Babies and young children don't need sugary foods or additional sugar. The natural sugars found in fruits and vegetables are enough.

NUTS These are a no-no. They can provoke allergies and are also choking hazards.

COW'S MILK Delay the introduction of cow's milk until one year. Never give young children skimmed milk—they need the calories that the fat in whole milk provides.

EGGS Wait until after one year before introducing whole eggs. The same goes for products that contain eggs.

SHELLFISH It's best not to give shellfish until your child is two years old.

CITRUS FRUITS These can upset a baby's tummy. Always deseed fruit.

SEEDS AND RAW FOOD Avoid food that might cause choking, such as seeds or hard pieces of food. No raw food whatsoever.

Weaning

After your baby has got used to a small meal of a dozen spoonfuls once a day, you can start offering him food at other times as well. If you began by giving him food at lunchtime, you can now introduce breakfast.

Offer regular drinks of diluted baby juice or cooled boiled water, both with mealtimes and at other times of the day. You can use either a bottle or a plastic baby cup. With your baby's nutritional needs increasingly met by solid food and his thirst quenched with water or diluted juice, his demands for a milk feeding, breast or bottle, may start to tail off naturally until you are down to a feeding first thing in the morning and last thing at night.

Some babies abruptly wean themselves and start to show little interest in breast or bottle once solid food is well established. If you're bottle-feeding, that's no problem, but if you're breastfeeding and your milk supply has not decreased, this can leave you with painfully engorged breasts for a few days. Expressing milk is not the answer, as it will only serve to stimulate the supply in the way the baby's sucking does. Wearing a well-fitting nursing bra night and day can help, and so can aloe vera gels.

More often, a breastfed baby will continue to want a "feeding" even when your supply of milk is next to nothing. In this case, what she wants is the continued comfort of the breast, not the milk itself. Essentially what she's doing is using the nipple as a pacifier.

If you want to stop breastfeeding and your child has settled into eating solid food and is taking enough fluids from a cup or bottle, cut the feedings right down, to two if possible. Then look out for a time when she skips one of those feedings and don't offer her the breast again. For many mothers, this is a real emotional stepping-stone. But there are gains to be made—your child is ready for a new stage and so are you.

After six to eight months, your baby needs more nutrients than bottle milk can give her. By carrying on feeding round the clock, you may be filling her up so much she doesn't have an appetite for the solid food you're introducing.

Some parents find weaning a bit of a juggling act. There's no hard and fast rule that can be applied to every child or parent—but if you have your mealtimes in place, there's no reason why you won't get there in the end.

Toddlers

Between the ages of one and a half and two and a half, a toddler is perfectly capable of eating and digesting most of what the rest of the family eats, provided it is mashed or cut up small enough. As the months pass, he also becomes increasingly able to feed himself, using a spoon and training cup.

You may notice that your child eats well at some times but not at others, or that she has a better appetite at lunch than at dinner. If that's the case, adjust things to suit, giving her more at lunchtime and a lighter meal in the evening. Be adventurous in what you offer her. Introduce a wide variety of foods at an early stage.

Food refusal can also be a feature of this age. When parents are faced with food refusal, their anxiety levels soar. They try to force their child to eat, and when this fails, as it is bound to do, they start to offer choices. When food is constantly refused, they allow cookies and other snacks they know their child will eat. just to ensure she's getting some form of food intake.

Once toddlerhood is well underway, your child will catch on that mealtimes provide a golden opportunity for getting attention. He'll clamp his mouth shut and turn his head away when the spoon approaches, and its contents will land in his ear. He'll go off his favorite supper with no warning. "But you love pasta and cheese!" He'll beg for cookies and cakes between meals. And that means the Food War has begun in earnest.

A lot of difficulties over feeding can be avoided if you relax. If your child is running around full of energy and isn't wasting away, chances are she's getting what she needs. Eating one good meal a day and picking at food the rest of the time won't do her any harm if that's the case. If you carry on offering her a balanced diet that includes all the main food groups and resist the temptation to fill her up on sugary or fatty snacks that have little nutritional value, you may still find that some of her meals will end up in the garbage or in the fridge, but you'll have avoided turning food into an issue of control.

FEEDING TODDLERS:

★ As soon as your child starts to handle a spoon and a cup with something approaching control, let him. Meals will take longer and be messier, but this is the type of independence you should be encouraging. Offer finger foods where possible. Before he can handle a spoon properly, he'll find it much easier to manage small sandwiches, cut-up fish sticks, cooked matchstick carrots and toast soldiers with his fingers.

★ Three meals a day is an adult pattern of eating. By all means carry on offering your child meals at regular times, but be prepared to give her a snack at mid-morning and mid-afternoon. Fruit, yogurt, chunks of cheese, toast and juice are much better than cakes, cookies and chips.

★ Keep portions small. A two-year-old doesn't need anything like the amount of food that you would put in front of an adult. She finds a huge portion just as off-putting as you would. The size of a children's plate—roughly the size of a side plate—is a good indication of the right portion size.

★ Praise and encouragement go a long way at this stage. If she's had enough, don't force the issue.

★ Keep offering variety. You won't know your child absolutely adores rice or pita bread until you've given him the chance to try it. Don't turn your own dislikes into your kids' dislikes. You might not like cooking or eating a particular food, but that's no reason not to offer it to him.

★ Protein and complex carbohydrates such as whole-grain pasta, and bread, and potatoes, are good foods for young children (and adults too!) because they release energy gradually over a long period of time and don't result in the instant peaks and sudden troughs you get with food that has a high sugar content.

★ Don't spring mealtimes on your child. Remember a toddler has very little sense of time. Give warnings when it's getting near lunch or dinner so she has a chance to prepare herself for the shift in activity.

★ If your child is still drinking a lot of milk at this stage, it may be affecting her appetite for solid food. Offer water or juice instead of milk all the time. Make sure the juice is very diluted, otherwise that may also fill her up.

★ Many parents praise their children if they have second helpings. Don't. Having a second helping should not be associated in the child's mind with behaving well.

Managing mealtimes

In the early days, kids need a lot of help, encouragement and supervision at mealtimes. But they also enjoy the social side of things. As soon as your child is old enough to sit unsupported in a high chair, he should sit at the table for meals. As soon as he is big enough to sit on a chair at the table, let him. You can always use a booster seat to bring him up to the right height.

In an episode of the American series of *Supernanny*, I visited a family called the Baileys whose mealtimes were real battlegrounds. Six-year-old Jadyn had ants in her pants and wouldn't sit still. Her two-year-old brother Billy was still in a high chair, pushed to one side of the table. Because he wasn't getting enough attention, he really acted up. One of the first things we did was to get Billy a booster seat so he could sit at the table with the rest of the family. It made a real difference right from the start. In his "Big Boy" chair, Billy got the idea it was fun to be a big boy when it came to behaving at mealtimes, and his eating really improved.

ALL TOGETHER

Wherever possible, families should try to eat together at least once a day. If that isn't possible, and in busy families it often isn't, then you should set aside time on the weekend for a shared meal or two. During the week, if you need to feed your child or your kids before you eat with your partner, there's no reason why you shouldn't sit down with them and have a snack or a piece of fruit. It's a social occasion and the ideal time to start to teach your children manners.

Stick to your routine. Set times for meals are important. If you bring a mealtime forward one day and delay it the next, expect to see swings in your child's moods and behavior brought on by abrupt changes in blood sugar level. When your child is older, you can be more flexible. At that stage, half an hour's difference won't hurt.

Make it clear what the rules are. Kids should be expected to sit at the table, not take their food and eat it somewhere else— certainly not in front of the TV. They should stay at the table until you tell them it's time to leave. The only reason they should be allowed to leave before they're finished or before you say they're finished is to go to the toilet. They should also be expected to wash their hands before eating and to say "Please" and "Thank you."

But be realistic. Older children often finish their food faster than younger ones. They shouldn't be expected to sit for ages while your toddler takes his time over his supper. Nor should they be expected to remain at the table while adults have a long conversation.

Under the age of two or two and a half, most eating difficulties can be managed by avoiding trouble in the first place, by not allowing food to become a battleground and by having realistic expectations about the type and quantity of food your child will eat. Older toddlers and young children, however, may start to push at the boundaries in other ways. At this point, it's time to make the rules crystal clear and back them up with firm and fair control.

You can make mealtimes less fractious and also get across the message that they are shared, social occasions if you involve your toddler in some of the preparations. This can also help to prevent whining or an explosion in those key moments between announcing that supper is on its way and its arrival on the table.

Ask your child to help set the table. "Can you find three spoons, please?" This gives the chance to praise her. "Now find three forks, please." Or at table, ask your child to pass simple items, such as a napkin. Say "Please" and "Thank you" at every opportunity to set a good example.

THE FUSSY EATER

It's reasonable to expect children—and that includes toddlers—to express likes and dislikes when it comes to food. Food doesn't have to be especially exotic to arouse a passionate refusal. Some kids hate tomatoes. Some hate peas. Some loathe mushrooms. If you're honest, there are probably a few things you don't like yourself.

Forcing a child by whatever means to eat a food he just doesn't like is counterproductive. He's not going to suddenly like tomatoes because you've succeeded in getting him to eat half of one. He may hate them even more. A child with a particular dislike of a certain food is not a fussy eater. A child who won't eat tomatoes, peas, cheese, pasta, mushrooms, eggs, meat—or practically anything else—is.

Little children go through spells when they haven't got much of an appetite or when they like to eat pretty much the same sort of thing over and over. If you don't make a big deal out of it, you'll find that they're happy to eat food they had previously refused when their appetite returns, or that they will broaden their tastes when they're ready for a change. But a fussy eater is different. The list of foods he won't eat will get longer every day until he's living on jam sandwiches or plain pasta. And you're probably going to find that type of behavior repeated in other areas.

One fussy eater in the family is bad enough. But fussy eating can be catching. Before long, you might find yourself maneuvered into the position of having to cook three separate meals for your three fussy eaters. In all likelihood, the fussiness won't stop there. It will often extend to how the food is put on the plate and what plate it is put on. That's bad enough at home, but it makes going out to eat or eating at a friend's house almost impossible.

A fussy eater is using food to make her parents jump through hoops. When things get this extreme, it's almost always about control.

PREVENTION IS BETTER THAN CURE

After your child has had years of practice at fussy eating, it's very difficult to turn things around. At school, you can tell which kids are the fussy eaters. They're the ones with strangely packed lunches or ones full of treats. It's far better to watch out for signs that food is starting to become an issue of control and nip things in the bud while you can.

★ If your child takes a sudden dislike to a particular food, don't overreact. Let her eat what she wants of the rest of her meal and clear it away when she's finished without drawing attention to what she didn't touch. She may announce: "I hate peas!" Don't pay too much attention to the statement. Offer the rejected food again in a few days and you may find she has changed her mind about it now she has seen that her refusal to eat it the first time round got no attention. Toddlers aren't logical or consistent in their likes and dislikes.

★ Allow your child some leeway. If he consistently dislikes a particular food, you may have to cook him something different when you offer that food to the rest of your family. Facial expressions can tell you a lot. The dislike will register spontaneously.

★ Praise and encourage your child when he does eat. If you insist on "three more spoonfuls," follow it through. Three more spoonfuls means three, not two or one.

★ Sometimes it's not the taste of a certain food a child doesn't like, it's the texture. Try offering the same food in a different form to see if that makes a difference. Some kids love raw carrots, but don't like cooked ones; some hate roast potatoes, but love mashed. It doesn't matter—they're still eating carrots and potatoes.

★ Don't offer choices to toddlers and young children. This is just asking for trouble. As much as possible, everyone in the family should be given the same meal, not invited to choose from a menu. Five-year-olds who are good eaters can be offered a couple of options.

★ If your child won't eat what's put in front of him, don't make him sit there all afternoon until he "finishes his plate." Toddlers have master's degrees in stubbornness. Compromise. Ask him to eat "three more spoonfuls" and follow it through. Then let him get down. Whatever you do, don't clear his plate away and then offer him a treat or a snack. He must get the idea that if he doesn't eat what you have given him, nothing else is on offer. He won't starve. Trust me.

PROBLEM:
NOT STAYING AT THE TABLE

This is a problem that tends to surface in the older toddler and can quickly turn mealtimes into chaos. A child who bounces in and out of her seat, who runs off with her food to eat it in a place of her choosing, or who gets down halfway through a meal with her mouth full and disappears under the table is trying to test your limits every bit as much as the fussy eater.

For mealtimes to be shared, enjoyable, sociable family occasions, there have to be certain agreed-upon rules. And those rules, if necessary, need to be backed up by firm and fair control. There are good reasons why a child should eat at table. For a start, it encourages good posture and good manners—no child can learn manners if he's not sitting at the table. Secondly, it's much easier to clear up spills at the table than to try and scrape mashed potato off the back of the sofa. Thirdly, a child who eats on the move isn't giving his digestive system much of a chance and may even risk choking if he starts to run around with food in his mouth. Lastly, even a toddler is not too young to follow the rules you've set and appreciate that he is part of a family and not a law unto himself. He won't necessarily understand your explanations, but he will be much more relaxed once he knows there are rules. And so will mealtimes.

SOLUTION:
THE NAUGHTY STEP TECHNIQUE

Many parents don't introduce any form of discipline to mealtimes because they are so focused on getting their kids to eat that they are prepared to turn a blind eye to unacceptable behavior. Insisting that basic rules are followed may well result in a period where mealtimes get worse before they get better, but it is far better to go through that short period rather than to abandon all hopes of peaceful family meals in the future.

Simply telling a child that she has to sit at the table to eat her food can be enough to get the message across. For aggressive or defiant behavior, follow the Naughty Step Technique outlined on page 80 and you'll start to see improvements very quickly.

Be realistic when it comes to how long you expect your child to sit at the table. Fifteen minutes is probably as long as you can expect most children under five to stay at the table. If your child has genuinely finished his food and asks to leave, then let him. At the same time, don't rush or get impatient with slow eaters. Don't put pressure on your child, or you will make eating a source of anxiety.

PROBLEM:
EATING TOO
MANY SNACKS

This is really a case where the problem is entirely of a parent's making. If there are cookies, sweets, cakes, chocolate and chips within your child's reach, who can blame him if he helps himself? If you give in every time he begs for a snack, it's not his fault if he has no appetite for his dinner.

Children who are allowed to graze all day long on food that has little nutritional value are not going to find mealtimes easy. They won't be hungry and they'll be fixed on the idea of getting another snack as soon as they can. Drinks, cookies and sweets with high sugar content play havoc with a child's blood sugar levels. Immediately after she's eaten or drunk something very sweet, her blood sugar will soar and that rush of energy will be immediately obvious in a lot of running around and shouting. Quite soon after, she'll hit a sugar low—lower than it was before the snack—and you can look forward to whining, bad behavior or even a tantrum. Snacks that are very salty and contain a lot of saturated fat, like chips, may not result in such dramatic highs and lows, but they are no better for kids than they are for adults.

SOLUTION:
RESTRICT ACCESS
TO SNACKS

✸ If your child has a real problem with snacking, don't buy the snacks in the first place. Leave them in the supermarket. That way there's no argument.

✸ Don't keep snacks where kids can help themselves. Put snacks away in a "snack box" and put it well out of reach.

✸ If your child is hungry between meals or after a particularly energetic play session, offer healthy snacks, not quick sugar fixes.

✸ Don't use snacks to bargain with children. The odd sweet or bag of chips produced out of the blue is fine, because it's on your terms. But don't start using snacks as a means to coax your child to eat his food or to reward good behavior.

✸ Don't allow snacks close to mealtimes. Give your child plenty of warning that a meal's coming up.

PROBLEM:
BAD MANNERS

Until your child is at least four years old, she's probably not going to be able to manage both a knife and fork with any great skill. If she still eats as much with her fingers as she manages to get on the fork, it doesn't matter. You can, however, introduce a basic level of table manners—for example, you can teach her not to leave the table with her mouth full. When children are past the age of five, then you can start fine-tuning table manners.

Even young children should be expected to say "Please" and "Thank you." It's just basic manners. They should also be told in no uncertain terms that behavior like throwing food at the table is not acceptable. The first time a toddler hurls a sausage at his sister, someone is bound to find it funny, but try to resist showing any amusement. When an adult laughs, it confirms to a child that the behavior is okay. That will only encourage a repeat performance.

SOLUTION:
INSIST ON THE RULES

★ Make it clear how you expect your kids to behave at the table. Food throwing, arguments, screaming and shouting, hitting and other forms of bad behavior are unacceptable in any age group. If the offense is serious, aggressive, and is often repeated, use the Naughty Step Technique (see page 80).

★ Teach your children to say "Please" and "Thank you." If those words aren't part of your vocabulary, how can they learn?

★ Don't expect sophisticated table manners before your child can even handle a knife and fork properly.

MY TOP TEN RULES

TO SUM UP, HERE'S HOW MY TOP TEN RULES APPLY TO EATING PROBLEMS:

1. PRAISE AND REWARDS

Praise and encouragement are the best rewards. Don't wait for exceptionally good behavior—praise the good moments when they happen. Don't use snacks as bribes. Don't praise a child for eating a second helping.

2. CONSISTENCY

Stick to the same rules and follow them through. Make sure you and your partner are consistent. If you insist on "three more spoonfuls," don't change your mind under pressure and reduce it to two, or one. Don't give a child a snack if he hasn't eaten his meal—that's a mixed message and a half!

3. ROUTINE

Don't shift mealtimes around drastically. Meals are a cornerstone of your routine. When children are older, you can be a little more flexible. Half an hour earlier or later won't hurt.

4. BOUNDARIES

A set mealtime is an important boundary. So are agreed-upon rules for sitting at the table and basic behavior. Boundaries help you to take the emotional heat out of mealtimes.

5. DISCIPLINE

Don't discipline a child for not eating. Do discipline for unacceptable behavior at mealtimes, such as hitting, throwing food or refusing to sit at the table. Use the Naughty Step Technique.

6. WARNINGS

Give plenty of advance notice when a meal is coming up so your child has a chance to prepare for the change in activity. Don't expect her to settle down immediately at the table if she has been running round the garden. Allow a period for her to calm down first. Give an advance warning if she has been naughty, so she has the chance to correct her behavior.

7. EXPLANATIONS

When your child has behaved badly at the table, explain that the behavior is unacceptable and why. Don't, however, offer complex explanations to toddlers. The reasoning will just sail over their heads.

8. RESTRAINT

Ignore passing food fads. Fussy eating is about attention-seeking—ignore it. Keep offering variety, and don't allow your kids to write their own menus. At the same time, don't make your dislikes their dislikes.

9. RESPONSIBILITY

Encourage your toddlers to feed themselves, even if it takes longer and makes a mess. Teach them to say "Please" and "Thank you." Involve older kids in setting the table and other simple tasks.

10. RELAXATION

Mealtimes should be fun and sociable occasions. Try to eat together as a family as much as possible.

Social skills

One of the most important things a child needs to learn is how to get along with other people. Toddlers tend to see other people as annoying obstacles who keep standing in the way of what they want to do. It takes a while before any child can appreciate that other people have feelings, too, and that sharing, taking turns and being nice are good skills to have. In some ways, you can't rush things. But you can make it clear what the limits are and head your child in the right direction.

What you can do, at each and every stage, is join in and have fun with your child. Take the time to do that—forget about having a perfect house. Enjoy your child. Many parents just don't play with their kids enough, yet playing is how children learn all sorts of things, including how to get on with other people. I'd really like to encourage parents to forget about being embarrassed and to let their hair down and be silly with their children. Go into their world and let them lead the play.

Playing

Play is how kids have fun, but it's also how they learn. From the six-month-old baby exploring a rattle by putting it in her mouth, to the two-year-old trying to bang a round peg into the square hole of a shape-sorter, or the four-year-old lost in a world of make-believe, play has as much to do with finding out about the world and learning to get on with other people as it does with entertainment.

A child who isn't given enough opportunities to play is going to be bored. When he's bored, he'll be cross and frustrated, and then he'll start getting into trouble. At the same time, he won't be learning the things he could be learning from play—and I'm not just talking about the type of mental skills that "educational" toys are meant to give him. Kicking a football around the garden isn't just an excuse for letting off steam. Your child is also learning physical coordination and other motor skills at the same time. Puzzles and games where he has to sit down and concentrate will help increase his attention span, so that when he gets to nursery or school he won't be one of those children who can't sit still and listen. Role play, "let's pretend," and dressing up feed the imagination. Drawing and painting are an outlet for creativity and help a child gain fine motor skills.

BABIES

It starts at a very early age. Babies need stimulation. It's just as important to meet that need for stimulation as it is to feed her when she's hungry or to change her when she's wet. A baby lacks both the coordination and the mobility to explore the world without help from you. For example, if you prop a toy where she can see it, she will gain some basic stimulation from the color and shape. But if you leave it within her reach, she will eventually bat it and make it move. The first time she does that, it will be by accident. But that accident will very quickly get repeated and turned into a game. And that game has taught her how to make something move with her hand, which is the beginning of coordination.

As soon as your child can walk, play turns into a fascinating game of exploration. Everything is up for grabs. Giving your child safe ways of experiencing the variety around him will feed that desire to learn. This is a great time for improvisation: wooden spoons and saucepans, plastic cups—basically anything safe you can pull out of the kitchen cupboards—will keep him just as happy and teach him just as much as a load of expensive toys.

TODDLERS

By the time your child is a toddler, play is as much an opportunity for frustration as it is for delight and discovery. She wants to put the shape into that box, she's seen you do it; she's seen her brother do it, but she can't manage to do it herself. The answer is not to remove all the things that might frustrate her—because she will never learn what she needs to learn that way—but you can divert her with another toy that she might be able to manage better. Or you can do what I do and place your hands over hers and help her put the shape into the box. That way she will learn, but she will still feel like she's doing it herself.

Don't expect her to concentrate on one thing for very long at this stage, and don't expect to see her play with another child. She may play beside another child and hardly notice that he's there. If she does notice him, it will be to note the fact that he's playing with a very interesting-looking toy that she wouldn't mind playing with herself. The next minute, she'll have snatched it from him.

SHARED PLAY

Before kids get to the stage where they can play with other children properly, sharing and cooperating, they need adults to help them play, and that's where problems can arise. You've got things you need to do, and if your child is happily playing, you'll see that as the ideal time to get on with your chores. Your child, on the other hand, will see playtime as the ideal time to have fun with you. And as soon as you start to get busy with the chores, he'll make it clear that he'd like your attention—by acting up, if that's what it takes. You need to keep times for chores separate from playtime.

Young children don't really think about different activities as "play" and "work" the way their parents do. Everything has the potential to be fun, including helping you wash the car. So an ideal solution for this between-stage is to get them involved with what you're doing. I've explained the Involvement Technique in the chapter Setting Boundaries (page 76) and it's a really useful way of giving your child attention when you need to be doing something else. When your child is standing on a chair beside you, "helping" you wash the carrots, you're not being a slave-driver or making him do something he'll see as a chore. He'll be having the time of his life.

Kids need clear lessons in sharing and taking turns. Simple games where two or more can play help to teach them give and take. But don't just leave them to it. Sit down with them. Show them how the game works. Tell them what the rules are. They won't be able to play together properly unless you've taught them how. "Now it's Arthur's turn."

When they are playing nicely, leave them to it. Don't hover or breathe down their necks. They will develop their own relationship and sort out their own squabbles and bickering if you aren't constantly acting as a referee.

TOYS

Toys multiply—fast. It seems like only yesterday when you could fit all your baby's toys into a single basket or box. Now that a few birthdays and Christmases have come and gone, you know you've got a house somewhere if you could only find it under all those Legos.

Kids love toys, and parents love giving toys to their children. But just like anything else, toys can end up becoming things that kids learn to bargain with, fight over, beg for, and refuse to tidy up. Toys can become an Issue.

Many parents at some stage or another have given their kids toys because they feel guilty about not spending more time with them. Others routinely hand out new treats as either a bribe or reward for halfway decent behavior. None of this has much to do with playing or learning through play. It has a lot to do with your emotions. If you use toys in this way, you'll be setting up a situation where your child knows he can manipulate you.

TOY ROTATION

Small children need toys to play with, but they don't need expensive toys and they don't need every toy in the toyshop. It's not just a question of "learning to appreciate what they've got." Older kids do need to be taught to respect their belongings, but that's much too grown-up a notion for a two-year-old. When small children find themselves in the position where they're surrounded by hundreds of toys, all within reach, what they're facing is literally hundreds of choices in solid form. They may have lots of toys, but they don't all have to be out at the same time. Rotating toys in and out of view gives small children, who can't choose between too many options, the chance to focus a little better on their play and develop their powers of concentration. They won't feel so overwhelmed by what's on offer. At a later date, you can bring out the toys you have put away, and they will greet them with as much excitement as if they were new. An added advantage of this strategy is that tidying up will be much easier.

TIDYING UP

When your home looks like a bomb-site two minutes after you've tidied up, the temptation can be to leave it that way. Many parents, faced with the never-ending struggle to put things away or get their kids to pick up after themselves, decide it's easier to live with chaos for the time being. The trouble is that the chaos sometimes lasts for years. It doesn't have to be that way—and it shouldn't be that way.

Some parents leave the mess because they don't want to spend time tidying up. What they forget is that mess itself is time-consuming and can even be expensive, if you're going to have to spend hours looking for missing pieces of jigsaws or fork out more money to buy new ones. A chaotic messy environment tells children that they don't have to respect their belongings. It also tells them that they don't have to respect yours.

When there are toys spread over every surface, your child will find it difficult to accept that there is anywhere in the home or anything in the home you might want to call your own. I've also noticed that mess makes discipline almost impossible to enforce. I'm not saying you should keep things neat as a pin and rush around constantly plumping up the cushions. But basic order is essential—kids can't learn anything when they're surrounded by chaos.

You can't expect a toddler to be tidy or to clean up after herself. But you can get her to join in when you tidy up—another good use for the Involvement Technique. Plenty of praise works wonders. The toy doesn't have to be in the right box. All the toys don't have to be picked up. Simply making it fun and getting them to join in lays down a good foundation for later. Sort different types of toys or equipment into different colored boxes—she'll find it easier to help that way. Make it a game: "Who can pick up the fastest?" Older kids need to know that you have rules about mess and that there are places in the home where you don't want toys underfoot all the time.

Here's how to cope:

★ Make tidying up into a game. Involve your child and give him praise when he helps.

★ Don't set unreasonably high standards.

★ Save yourself extra work by not allowing every single toy to be out at once. Rotate toys in and out of view.

★ Keep art materials, pens, markers and paints well out of reach. Supervise messy or creative play in an area where cleaning up is easy.

★ Explain the rules about tidying up, but don't expect perfection.

★ You can leave toys out in a playroom all day, or even tidy up every other day. You can always close the door on the chaos. But don't leave the mess for months.

How much TV?

"Far too much" is the answer in many cases. In some homes, the TV is on all day, morning, noon and night. Kids who watch TV round the clock aren't getting healthy exercise, they aren't using their imaginations, and they aren't interacting with each other. What they are getting is mindless stimulation that will wind them up, shorten their attention spans, and give them all sorts of ideas that you would rather they didn't have. I'm not just talking about exposure to violence or bad language, I'm talking about the ads that will whet their appetite for food you don't want them to eat or toys you can't afford.

It's almost as bad if the TV is on and no one's watching it. All it's doing is adding to the noise levels and general confusion.

Here's how to manage your kids' viewing:

- You need to be the boss of the remote control. Decide how long you are prepared to allow your kids to watch TV and decide which programs are suitable. In the case of older children, you can involve them in the choice.

- Don't use the TV as a babysitter. It's not the answer to child care or time management. But if you pop your child in front of *Snow White* on the video to get an extra half hour in bed on Saturday morning, don't beat yourself up about it. You're not the only one. And it's perfectly acceptable to put a video on for your little boy while you sit on the sofa and breastfeed his sister. Just use the TV wisely.

- Don't allow children to watch noisy cartoons or play computer games in the time leading up to bed. It makes them over-excited and overstimulated.

- Don't let your kids watch programs that scare them. Even children's films and cartoons can be scary for some children. Keep an eye on what they're watching and how they react.

Tips for happy play

Variety is the spice of life. Keep activities varied, and you'll stand a better chance of keeping your kids happy. Play doesn't just mean toys—it means outings and trips to the park, running about in the garden, "helping" Mom and Dad with a job, creative fun with paints and Play-Doh, games of "let's pretend." Games don't have to be loud and boisterous. Quiet times can be just as much fun.

🧸 Let your child choose what she wants to play.

🧸 Encourage your child to work things out for herself. Show her how, but let her do it. That's how she learns.

🧸 Let your hair down. Don't be serious about play. Be silly, join in and enjoy yourself. Let your child direct the play.

🧸 When rain stops outdoor play and you and your kids feel cooped up, improvise play. Make them a "den" or a "tent" using old sheets and blankets draped over a table or a sofa.

🧸 Let your child's imagination run riot. Dressing-up clothes are great for role play. Give her your old clothes to have fun with.

🧸 Don't push a child into playing with a toy that is too old for her. It won't speed up her development, and it will only frustrate her. Toys and games come with recommended ages not just for reasons of safety.

🧸 Don't buy expensive breakable toys for children who are too young to be careful. You're just giving yourself something else to worry and nag about, and you'll only end up blaming your child when the toy does get broken. And that's not fair on the child. Expense means nothing to a small child. It certainly does not mean a better toy. Think of all the fun a two-year-old can have with wrapping paper and empty boxes.

🧸 Get outside whenever you can. Kids need room to breathe and space to run around and get rid of their excess energy. You need it too!

PROBLEM:
FIGHTING/AGGRESSIVE BEHAVIOR

Play can sometimes bring out the worst in kids. One minute they're playing nicely, and the next, World War Three has just broken out in the living room.

Hostilities can erupt for all sorts of reasons. In toddlers, it's often unthinking. A young toddler will act on impulse unless he is diverted or prevented from doing so. He won't know that kicking someone will hurt. It just seemed like a good idea for the nanosecond it flashed through his head. Young kids sometimes lash out physically because they can't resolve things in words.

Older toddlers quickly learn that fighting, biting and other kinds of aggressive behavior get them instant attention. It's negative attention, but it's better than none at all. Jealousy can also be to blame, as well as a shaky grasp of sharing and cooperation. Losing a game or refusing to hand over a toy can trigger an outburst of violent fury.

Bear in mind that there's a difference between the odd skirmish, quarrel or squabble, and out-and-out fighting. Don't rush in at the first sign of an argument. Let them see if they can sort it out for themselves. Fighting and aggression is different.

It's important to understand the reasons that lie behind fighting and aggression, but it's equally important to make it clear that you just won't tolerate it. Any child who gets away with aggressive behavior in the home will get the idea that the same thing is acceptable at her friend's house, in the park, and at nursery or school.

SOLUTION:
THE NAUGHTY STEP TECHNIQUE

Fighting and aggression in young toddlers should be nipped in the bud. As soon as your child shows that she is old enough to understand what she's doing, use the Naughty Step Technique (see page 80) to show her that this kind of behavior is just not allowed. There's no two ways about it. Fighting means zero tolerance. Use the One-Strike-And-You're-Out Technique (page 84) in the case of an older child who really should know better.

When fighting is constantly happening at playtime, you need to make sure your child understands what shared play is all about. After the discipline is over, sit down and play with your kids and show them how to take turns.

PROBLEM:
DESTRUCTIVE BEHAVIOR

If you give a baby a book with paper pages, the next time you look, some of those pages might be chewed, crumpled, torn, sucked, or otherwise investigated. That's not destructive behavior. If your young toddler has knocked into a table and sent an ornament flying, that's not destructive behavior, either. It's an accident (and an oversight on your part). If your four-year-old is tearing the wallpaper off his bedroom wall and scribbling on the doors with felt tips; if he breaks a toy ten minutes after he's been given it—that's destructive behavior.

SOLUTION:
TEACHING RESPECT

Make sure your child understands the rules. Explain that writing on the walls, ripping wallpaper, or breaking toys is just not allowed. Use the Naughty Step Technique (see page 80) to back up your rules. In extreme cases, you might want to use the Toy Confiscation Technique (page 86) and limit his toys to ten until he learns how to play nicely with them and look after them.

At the same time, take a good hard look at your home. If it's total chaos, your child won't get the message that it's important to respect his surroundings and his belongings. To enforce discipline on this issue and on most other issues, too, you don't need a show home, but you do need a basic degree of order.

Other behavioral issues

Parenting throws up lots of gray areas. It's not a gray area when your child spits or throws food; it's not a gray area if he hurts another child. But what about whining and complaining? What about shyness?

Children are little copycats, and they pick things up fast. Before they set foot in a school playground for the first time, you can't very well blame bad language on other kids. They're most likely to have heard those naughty words coming from you—even worse, the first time they come out with them, it's bound to be in front of someone you'd least like to hear them. Your parents, for example.

First, look at your own behavior. You can't set standards for children in the abstract. You can't say one thing and do the other and expect them to do what you say. Positive reinforcement in the form of praise for good behavior can go a long way to correcting these kind of "gray area" issues.

PROBLEM:
WHINING

Kids pick up everything. If you spend a lot of time complaining, chances are your child is bound to pick up the tone and start to use it on you. That drip-drip-drip is designed to wear you down until you give up and give him what he wants.

SOLUTION:
DON'T GIVE IN

Don't give in to whining. Giving in teaches a child that whining is the sort of behavior and tone of voice that will guarantee a result. If your child is whining for something you don't want her to have, explain that a) you aren't going to give her the cookie because it's nearly lunchtime and that b) whining is not the way to ask for things.

If she is whining for something she can have, explain that she can have it as soon as she asks for it properly. Show and tell her how you want her to behave:

"Don't whine for juice." Copy her whining face and tone. Every time I do that with children, they collapse in fits of giggles. It gets the message across.

Then tell her how to ask properly. "You can have some juice when you ask for it politely. Say, 'Please can I have some juice?' Now you say it."

PROBLEM:
SHYNESS

Babies and toddlers are often shy of people they don't know. This is natural, and it's a feature of that stage where a child is very attached to her mother or her prime caregiver and is anxious about any form of separation. It's not really shyness. Don't pay too much attention to it and try to resist the temptation to label your child as "shy," or even worse, to think that her behavior is "sweet."

It's okay if your kid is a little shy. There's nothing wrong with it. Some children are naturally more outgoing than others. But extreme shyness in older children can cause difficulties when you invite people over or go to your friends' houses. If you don't come to grips with it, it may end up causing problems when your child starts in school.

Some children use shy behavior as a way of getting attention, or to get out of doing something they don't want to do. Those are the ones clinging to Mom's skirt while Mom makes desperate attempts to get them to say hello to someone they know perfectly well.

SOLUTION:
SHOW AND TELL

Don't make a fuss about shyness and give your child more attention than he would otherwise have got. Show and tell him how you expect him to behave with other people. Coax his confidence along in a light-hearted way. From a young age, expose your child to situations where he is surrounded by other people, especially other children.

Teach him that it's nice and polite to say "Hello" to other people. Explain new situations before your child encounters them so he won't react by hanging back. Let him see you move confidently around other people—at the park, in your friend's home, at playgroup—and don't let him draw you into his own shy little corner.

PROBLEM:
FEARS

Small children are frightened by lots of things:
nightmares, loud noises, water, dogs,
witches, and other products of their busy
imaginations. Always take fears seriously.
They're very serious to the child.

Some fears are associated with certain
ages. Many children around a year to two
years old hate the sound of the vacuum
cleaner and other domestic machines like
food processors. When children get to four or
thereabouts, they often become scared of
dogs. Irrational fears are a feature of the
stage when there's no clear line between
fantasy and reality. That doesn't mean the
fear is any less real.

A child may also have a nightmare if he's
seen something scary on TV. Even cartoons
and Disney films can scare some kids. Keep
an eye on what's he watching and how he's
reacting—and switch it off if he seems to be
getting upset.

EXPLANATION AND REASSURANCE

When your child is frightened, the first thing she needs is your reassurance and comfort. Explanations can go a long way. Fears like being scared of the vacuum will usually pass by themselves. In the meantime you can help things along by gradually getting her used to the sound of a vacuum or blender or whatever appliance is frightening her. Bring her into the room with you, but keep her a good distance away from the appliance. Tell her you're going to use the vacuum. Switch it on and off quickly a few times so she can hear the noise stop as well as start. Then use the appliance, but keep your distance from your child. It's being close to the sound that panics her.

Other fears—like fear of water or fear of dogs—need to be handled by introducing the child gradually and in a subtle way to what's scaring him so he can learn to relax and get over the fear. Try to put yourself in his shoes. Viewed from an adult height, a dog might not be particularly scary. A four-year-old is seeing a much bigger picture of the same animal, and it's right in his face. Once he has relaxed, instead of climbing on your shoulder to bury his face in your neck, he'll be on the floor and his own two feet.

Never doubt a child the first time she comes to wake you reporting a nightmare. She needs to feel she can talk to you about what's scaring her. You've got to keep the lines of communication open and not dismiss her fears.

If it's nighttime and your child has had a nightmare or has woken up and imagined something scary, take her back to bed and give her comfort and reassurance. She might have got frightened by the strange shape a toy made in the dark. Sit with her, with the lights off, and show her that the silhouette is just her favorite doll. Leave the door ajar and the hall light on. When she has settled down, tell her where you'll be and what you'll be doing: "I'm just going to be downstairs if you need to talk to me. I'm going to have my supper and then I'm going to watch TV." Tuck her in with her favorite cuddly toys and soothers.

Out and about

Kids really do choose their moments. They reserve some of their worst behavior for situations where it's going to embarrass you the most, and that means in full public view. That's not surprising. Your child can read you like a book, and will have picked up the signals that you're stressed, tense or anxious before you even leave the house. You might even have made it especially easy for him by telling him that you don't want him to act up. "We're going to the supermarket, and this time I want you to behave. Do you hear?"

If the embarrassment factor isn't bad enough, there's also the fear factor. Walking down the street or driving in the car with small children are potentially dangerous situations. Before a child is old enough to appreciate the importance of safety, a rule about a seat belt is just another restriction that she might decide to test to the limit.

PROBLEM:
SUPERMARKET SHOPPING

Small children misbehave in supermarkets. They whine to get down from the cart, they run off down the aisles, they pull things off shelves, they beg for treats and—when all else fails—they have a tantrum at the checkout.

Many parents live in absolute dread of the weekly supermarket shopping. Or of any shopping expedition. Some dread it so much that they never take their kids with them.

It just isn't always practical to arrange your shopping expeditions around the times when your kids can be looked after by someone else. There are better ways to use those occasions—on quality time for yourself and your partner, for example.

SOLUTION:
THE INVOLVEMENT TECHNIQUE

You might find the weekly shopping a chore, but you don't need to communicate that fact to your toddler. Children act up in supermarkets because they're bored, you're busy and distracted, and they know that gives them the perfect opportunity to misbehave.

The solution, which works wonders with toddlers and small children, is to involve your child in what you're doing. Make it exciting for him. Give him tasks to do.

When I take a child to the supermarket, I make her a little shopping list of her own. I have a big list and she has a mini list, with a few things on it that she is in charge of getting. These are proper adult things, like bread, milk, oranges and juice. While we're going up and down the aisles, I keep reminding her of what's on her list and telling her to look out for them. "Have you seen the milk yet?"

You can draw pictures instead of writing words on the "mini" list if you like, but I find that even small children can remember a short list of three or four things. Make sure you include something to find at the beginning of the shop, something from the middle aisles and something from the end so the game lasts the whole way round the supermarket.

On *Supernanny*, we tried this technique on Charlie, a two-and-a-half-year-old who had previously had plenty of experience in terrorizing supermarkets. The sequence wasn't included in the final program, but I can tell you the technique worked like a charm.

PROBLEM:
CAR JOURNEYS

The lowest level of problem you'll get in the car is the "Are we there yet?" variety, when your child makes it clear at ten-second intervals that the whole trip's taking far too long and he's fed up. He'll usually start on this refrain as soon as you turn out of your driveway.

If you've got more than one child in the back, boredom can lead to squabbling and bickering, fighting and kicking. In extreme cases, a child may try to escape from the car seat or unbuckle her seat belt.

Very occasionally, children will behave badly in the car because they're frightened of that particular situation. Sometimes, the problem may be caused by carsickness. Before your child can communicate clearly to you that traveling in a car (or a train for that matter) makes her feel sick, the first indication you'll have (after the screaming and crying) is an ashen gray face, immediately before she actually is sick. Ask your doctor or pharmacist for motion sickness remedies if you suspect that carsickness is at the root of the problem. It can make children really miserable. Make sure your car is not too hot and stuffy. That can make children queasy. There are also strips you can buy that hang underneath the car from the axle and drag along the road. By grounding the car, these help prevent carsickness.

SOLUTION:
DISTRACTION AND INVOLVEMENT

Try to preempt bad behavior in the car by making journeys interesting and exciting in themselves, not just a means to an end. Get your child to choose a favorite toy to play with in the car. Play audio books and cassettes. Point out interesting things out of the window. You can get older kids to play simple spotting games—"How many red cars can you see?"—and "I spy with my little eye" is another good one.

If your child persists in acting up in the car or has managed to escape from his child seat or seat belt, pull over at the first safe opportunity. Unrestrained children are in real danger in cars, which is why it's illegal for them not to be belted in a child seat. Put him back in his seat, buckle him up, resisting the stiff legs, arching back and tantrum that might result, and wait until he is calm before setting off again. Explain very sternly how important it is that he stays in his seat.

PROBLEM:
RUNNING OFF

For every clingy toddler, there's one who just loves to give you the slip—in the park, on the street, in the shop. One minute he's holding your hand, and the next minute your heart is in your mouth. To him, it's an exciting game of chase, or hide and seek on a grand scale. To you, until you find him again unharmed, it's potentially the worst-case scenario.

SOLUTION:
RULES AND EXPLANATIONS/REINS

Make it very clear that your child is to hold your hand at all times when you are crossing the road. Explain why. Teach her in a positive way and get her to rehearse the reasons each time you come to a crossing. "Now what do we do? We hold hands. We look out for cars. We look both ways, and when it's safe we cross the road." You can't repeat it often enough. "Look for the green (or white) man. Can you see the green man? When you see the green man, that means it's safe to cross the road."

When you take your child to the park or somewhere similar, explain carefully how far he can go. "Stay around the slide where I can see you." Build up trust. If he runs off, bring him back and make him hold your hand, hold the stroller, or sit in it. It's like pulling on imaginary reins.

But if you have a toddler on your hands who is determined to run off at every opportunity, rules and explanations won't work. If your anxiety has got the better of you, I don't see any reason why you shouldn't use real reins in this situation. It will make you feel better, at least. Until he gets to the age when he's got a bit of common sense and can control his impulse to run off, it's better to be safe than sorry.

MY TOP TEN RULES

TO SUM UP, HERE'S HOW MY TOP TEN RULES APPLY TO SOCIAL SKILLS AND BEHAVIOR PROBLEMS:

1. PRAISE AND REWARDS

Praise and positive reinforcement are important when it comes to teaching social skills. Notice good behavior. Don't use toys as treats on a regular basis.

2. CONSISTENCY

Don't change or make up rules as you go along. Follow through and make sure your partner backs you up. Constantly reinforce important rules, like those about crossing the road safely.

3. ROUTINE

Build time into your schedule for play, indoors and out. Vary play activities, and have special treats or games up your sleeve for days when rain stops play. Try to get outdoors as much as possible to let children blow off steam.

4. BOUNDARIES

Be clear about your rules and what you expect in terms of behavior. Set limits on TV watching. Teach respect for possessions by keeping chaos under control. Don't give in to whining.

5. DISCIPLINE

Use the Naughty Step Technique for unacceptable behavior like fighting and aggression.

6 WARNINGS

Give warnings about what's happening next so your child can prepare herself. Don't interrupt play suddenly and expect your child to move smoothly on to the next activity. Give warnings before disciplining so she can correct her behavior herself.

7 EXPLANATIONS

Show and tell your child how you expect him to behave when it comes to "gray areas." Always talk over the reasons behind fears, and give plenty of reassurance. Teach your children how to play games and how to play with toys.

8. RESTRAINT

Don't buy your child the entire contents of the toy shop. Improvised toys are just as much fun. Practise toy rotation so that everything's not out at once. Take control of the TV and monitor what your children are watching.

9. RESPONSIBILITY

Teach your child how to share and take turns. Don't always hover over your kids when they play. Use the Involvement Technique for supermarket shopping and at other times when you need to be busy.

10. RELAXATION

Enjoy your children. Get involved in their play and let them direct it. Cuddle up with them and read them a story.

Bedtime

Remember sleep? Remember getting into bed, snuggling down beside your partner *and sleeping through the night*? Remember waking up, refreshed and ready for the day? A good night's sleep is a distant memory for many parents of small children. But it doesn't have to be that way.

I think it's fair to say that sleeping problems send more parents in search of support and advice than any other child care issue. That's not surprising. Of all the family battlegrounds and crisis points, difficulties at bedtime have the potential to cause the greatest distress. From the baby who cries off and on all night, to the boisterous toddler whose idea of a good game is to spin out bedtime until midnight, to the preschooler plagued with night terrors who creeps into your bed hours before dawn, sleep problems take many forms and can occur at any age.

If your child doesn't sleep, or sleeps poorly; if it takes the whole evening just to put your child to bed; everyone is going to suffer. Anyone can bounce back after the odd broken night, but weeks and weeks of lost evenings or disturbed rest amount to pure torture. When you're that exhausted, the simplest task becomes an uphill struggle. Without regular sleep, even the happiest, most easygoing person will be irritable, depressed, less able to concentrate and more likely to have accidents or fall ill. If that zombie-like state isn't bad enough, you'll also find it harder to cope with your child during the daytime, and you'll lose your patience, which will mean more clashes, more tantrums and frayed nerves all round.

And the effects ripple outward. One wakeful little body and you'll not only have an exhausted Mom, but a worn-out Dad and irritable older children, too—in other words, an entire household running on empty. Last but not least, despite all appearances to the contrary, your sleepless child will also suffer. It may not seem that way, but the bright-eyed toddler bouncing off the walls at 4 A.M. is not getting the rest he needs. Unlike adults or older kids, a toddler or young child who gets to sleep late or wakes up for long periods during the night is not usually able to catch up on that sleep.

The good news is that even the worst sleep problems can be turned around in a surprisingly short space of time. It may take only a few days. Once you've sorted out a proper sleep pattern for your child, you won't look back. I have used the techniques outlined in this chapter countless times with success. They work. And the benefits are immediate, for everyone in the household. You'll be amazed to find your child not only sleeping through the night, but taking regular daytime naps, too. You'll probably notice that her appetite also improves. Daytimes will be calmer, and you'll begin to enjoy your child much more.

As with any rule or technique, you have to stick with it. At the end of the day, when you're tired, or in the middle of the night, when you've just stumbled from a warm bed, it's easy to let things slide. All parents are programd to respond to crying, but there is a difference between genuine distress and the type of crying whose purpose is to wear you down so that you give in. Remember: you're not being mean. You are simply teaching your child how to get what all kids need, which is a good night's sleep. He doesn't know he needs to sleep, but you do. And you know best.

PROBLEM:
REFUSING
TO GO TO BED

The child who refuses to go to bed is depriving himself of much-needed sleep, and you of much-needed quality time that you could be spending on yourself, your partner, or your other kids. This may not be as serious as the exhaustion that results from repeated waking in the night, but it is a major source of irritation and tension in many families. A milder version of the same problem is where the child asks for umpteen drinks of water or trips to the toilet, and indulges in similar delaying tactics in an attempt to fend off the inevitable moment of separation.

Toddlers who have gained the upper hand in other areas of family life are particularly prone to this type of behavior; for many kids, bedtimes can continue to be battlegrounds for years to come.

SOLUTION:
THE BEDTIME
ROUTINE

A bedtime routine has two important functions. It lets your child know that there is a consistent pattern to going to bed, which she is not going to be able to change or manipulate at will, and it prepares her for sleep in a calming sequence of events that are designed to help her relax.

A sensible bedtime

The first step is to set a time for going to bed. Whatever time young children are put to bed, they tend to wake up at the same time in the morning—generally fairly early, and sometimes as soon as it gets light. That means the later they go to bed, the more tired they will be the next day. The whole notion of sleeping in is alien to under-fives.

In my experience, most kids of preschool age benefit from a bedtime of 7:00 to 8:00 P.M. Once the bedtime routine has been put into practice, many parents who have previously reported that their child seems to need less sleep than others their age are often surprised to find their wakeful toddler happily going to bed much earlier than they expected and sleeping for longer.

However, at some point between the ages of two and four, the blissful interval of the afternoon nap will be outgrown. Parents of young children understandably treasure that brief window of sanity, when they can have a shower, a cup of tea or simply enjoy the sound of silence. But you can't reasonably expect this stage to last forever. If you start to find bedtimes getting difficult again and your child doesn't seem particularly sleepy despite all your soothing strategies, it may be time for the nap to become a thing of the past. Inevitably, there may be a period of transition, when your child is too wakeful at bedtime if she has a nap in the afternoon, but overtired and fractious if she doesn't have one. Trust me, it's short-lived.

A set bedtime gives small children the rest they need. It gives older siblings an extra hour or so when they can call on your attention—for a chat, for help with homework, or just to be with you. And it gives you and your partner your evenings back.

HOW TO SPOT A SLEEPY CHILD

If bedtimes in your household are war zones, you may be missing the signs that tell you your child is ready for bed, whatever they are saying to the contrary. A yawn is a dead giveaway, of course, but other signs include whining and fractious behavior (the whole "tears before bedtime" scenario) as well as rubbing eyes, thumb sucking and flopping on the floor. If your child shows such signs much earlier than the bedtime you have set, you can move your schedule forward; if the signs are delayed, you can move it back by small steps each day.

Countdown to bed

You've set a bedtime. It's posted up there on the wall as part of your family timetable. Now you have to put it into practice.

The key to an effective bedtime routine is to allow just enough time for each stage so the child does not feel like he is being rushed into things, but not so much that he starts to get the idea that all of a sudden there is room to maneuver. About an hour from getting into the bath to saying good-night is about right.

Unless your child is very precocious, she's not going to have any idea what an hour feels like. Children have only very sketchy notions of time. It's your job to be the Speaking Clock:

"In five minutes, it's time to get into the bath."

"In two minutes, it's time to get out of the bath."

"After I read you this story, it's time to put out the light."

Easing the child through the bedtime routine means giving regular notice about what's coming next so the child has time to prepare for each stage. In some ways, this works a little bit like the verbal warnings you give for bad behavior, except there's no disapproval attached.

HOW TO PUT YOUR CHILD TO BED:

In the time leading to bedtime, keep things as calm as possible. This is not the time for noisy cartoons and videos, computer games or rough and tumble. An overstimulated, overexcited child can't just switch off and go to sleep any more than an adult can. Winding down is important.

Give a clear indication that bedtime is approaching about ten minutes before you start the routine.

Begin with a bath. Warm water is a natural aid to relaxation. Give a warning before the bath begins and before it's about to finish.

Enlist the child's cooperation over simple tasks. It will help her feel involved. "Now it's time to get out of the bath. Can you pull out the plug for me? Well done!"

Praise the child when each stage is completed smoothly.

Read your child a bedtime story. Let her choose one from a small selection. Don't offer too much choice or you might get locked into a battle of wills, but if she has a favorite story, by all means read that (and be prepared to read it the next night, and the night after that, and the night after that...). Ask her questions about the pictures to engage her attention. "Can you see the rabbit? What's the rabbit doing?"

You may find that after the story, he wants to talk for a little while. This is a good time for reassurance, praise, and for singling out good moments. "You were a very good boy at lunch today." You might also want to tell him what's going to be happening tomorrow. "We're going to the park with Rose, and then we're going to Izzie's for tea."

A few comforters or soft toys can all help ease the separation of bedtime, but don't turn the bed into a playpen. When you sneak back to check on her later, you can put a few toys at the bottom of the bed in case she wakes up early and wants to play.

As the time for "lights out" approaches, give a few minutes' notice.

Don't get into the habit of waiting with your child until she falls asleep. If she's tired and you've been through the routine step by step, she should be fairly drowsy by now and will drift off easily.

Lights out! No child can learn how to get to sleep with the light on.

Don't be tempted to take a shortcut and rush the routine. If you leave out a stage, your child will notice and you'll lose his cooperation. That way, it will probably end up taking even longer.

If you're taking turns with your partner to put your child to bed, make sure you both follow the same rules and stages. Be consistent and present a united front.

Don't let your child fall asleep on the sofa and then move him into bed. He'll wake up in a panic wondering how he got there.

Managing multiple bedtimes

Older kids can manage many of the bedtime stages with minimal supervision. But if you have more than one child under five, bedtime is still very much a hands-on affair. The more kids you have, the more hands you're going to need.

The answer is to split or stagger the bedtimes so that the younger goes to bed first, shortly followed by the older child. If at all possible, divide your efforts so that one parent is reponsible for one child, while the other parent looks after the other one. Bedtime works best when each child gets some degree of individual attention. Make sure you swap things around the next night so that each child has a chance to have a special time with Mom and Dad.

Where multiple bedtimes can usefully overlap is bathtime. You can enlist the help of your older child when it comes to bathing her younger sibling. Simple tasks like fetching the soap or washcloth, and getting a towel or toy, can boost a child's confidence and willingness to cooperate. This type of involvement often has a repeating effect, making her much better behaved when it comes to her own bedtime routine.

Disrupted routines

There are two types of disruption that can play havoc with routines: those that are avoidable and those that are not. By all means allow your children to stay up a little later on Saturday, provided you're prepared to stand your ground and enforce regular bedtime on Sunday night. But don't allow yourself to be talked into allowing a child to stay up to watch a television program. That's what the video is for.

However, there are times when a routine goes out of the window. When a child is ill or teething, physical discomfort will inevitably overrule any soothing strategy. Once the crisis has past, get back to the routine as soon as possible. Don't allow the interruption to become an excuse to relax the rules.

Children identify very strongly with their own beds, and derive great security from familiar surroundings, which often makes it difficult to settle them when you are away from home. Reminders of their own bed and bedroom can be useful comforters in a strange setting—take favorite toys and blankets. Try to stick to a similar routine when you're away as much as possible, so that you don't have to reinvent the wheel when you get home.

PROBLEM:
NOT BEING ABLE TO GET TO SLEEP ALONE

If you've always waited until your child has fallen asleep before you leave the room, your presence will be built into her notion of bedtime and she's going to find the moment of separation particularly difficult. And you're going to find that large chunks of your evening are vanishing without trace.

Children who can get to sleep only with a parent in the room need to learn how to fall asleep by themselves. What might start as a little extra comfort when the child is very little can turn into an issue of control as the child learns how to put off the moment of separation longer and longer to keep you by their side.

SOLUTION:
THE SLEEP SEPARATION TECHNIQUE

This technique is a means of gradually breaking the cycle of dependency, so your child learns that he can get to sleep without your being in the room.

★ When you put your child to bed, don't get into bed with him. Don't sit on the bed. Say good-night, give him a cuddle and tell him it's time to go to sleep. Then sit very close to the bed on the floor.

★ Turn the child so he's facing away from you. If he keeps eye contact with you, he will try to start a conversation. Tell him to close his eyes and that it's time to go to sleep.

★ Make sure the light is off and the door is open.

★ Sit in silence, not looking at the child, until the child goes to sleep. Each time he tries to talk to you, just tell him, "Sleep."

★ The next night, repeat the same stages, sitting a little further away from the bed. Over the coming nights, move further and further toward the door until you are sitting outside the open door.

★ The last stage is to go through the procedure sitting outside the door, with the door ajar. Naturally this technique is going to take quite a while, but remember that you're breaking a habit that could otherwise go on for years.

PROBLEM:
WAKING IN THE NIGHT

All children, and adults, too, have brief periods of wakefulness throughout the night. Every hour or so we come to the brink of consciousness, then turn over and drift back to sleep. That's part of a natural sleep pattern. What isn't natural is when that brief wakeful period leads to full consciousness and the inability to settle back into sleep.

Everyone has experienced nights like that. You may find yourself wide awake at 3 A.M., unable to switch off your anxieties over a looming deadline or an unforeseen expense. Or you may have awakened to the sound of your neighbors throwing the party of a lifetime next door, and find you can't tune out the noise and get back to sleep again. Fears, nightmares, and things that go bump in the night can also wake children, as can the discomfort of teething or illness. But persistent waking, over days and weeks, accompanied by crying and/or getting out of bed is a different story altogether. If you respond to night-waking by offering food, comfort and entertainment on demand, you will only reinforce a bad habit and your child won't learn how to settle by herself.

BABIES

Very young babies, particularly those who are breastfed, will wake at regular intervals throughout the night chiefly because they are hungry or wet. An infant can only take in so much milk at one time; when that's digested, your baby will be ready for more, and will soon let you know it.

When feeding is going on around the clock, interrupted sleep is inevitable, but there are various ways in which you can minimize the disruption to yourself and start to teach your baby the difference between day and night.

★ Use a night-light.

★ In the very early days, keep the baby's crib or basket in your room so you can respond before a whimper turns into a full-throated cry, waking everyone in the vicinity. However, I would suggest that you don't keep the baby in your room for too long. You may find yourself waking unnecessarily when she makes the slightest noise, and it may well make separation an issue later on. Three months is a suitable age to move a baby into her own room.

★ When the baby wakes, feed her, but don't talk to her or stimulate her with play. Get across the message that night is different from day. Burp her, change her diaper, and settle her down.

★ If your baby is sleeping, but you haven't gone to bed yet, don't tiptoe around the house trying to keep everything as quiet as possible. A sudden loud noise may wake a baby, but normal household sounds won't.

★ Share the load. If you are bottle-feeding, work out a rotation so that your partner shares some of the night feedings. If you are breastfeeding, express some milk.

Once the baby is fed, he may well fall asleep in your arms. If he doesn't, put him back into his crib and let him settle himself to sleep. If the whimpering carries on, try a gentle rub on the back or the tummy, but don't pick him up again unless he starts to cry in earnest. It may be gas that is bothering him, in which case, ease him over your shoulder and pat his back.

AFTER WEANING

After solid food is an established part of the diet, *there is no reason why a baby should not sleep through the night.* If he keeps waking up several times a night, night after night, it's not because of hunger, but for a different reason altogether, and that's usually to seek comfort.

If it isn't bad enough getting up every hour to see to a crying child, many parents then find themselves locked into hours of pacing or rocking with a wide-awake child over their shoulder. After a while, broken nights become the norm. A child who is picked up, fed and soothed every time she wakes and cries soon learns that there's more of the same where that came from. Let's face it, you don't want to be driving around the neighborhood in your pajamas, trying to get the child buckled in the car seat behind you to doze off.

If the night-waking is recent and has only lasted a few days, the cause may be teething. Sniffles and colds will also disrupt a baby's sleep. Rule out illness or teething first.

Bouts of wakefulness are sometimes caused when a child feels she has missed out on attention during the day, in which case it's a protest to let you know she feels short-changed. If you've been very busy or harried, think about ways you can spend more quality time with her during the day.

If the child is easily soothed by a reassuring back rub or a quick cuddle, you don't need to take further steps. The problem will sort itself out with time. Don't respond to every whimper: give him a chance to learn how to settle himself.

If you want to carry on breastfeeding past the introduction of solid food, restrict feedings to the daytime, last thing at night, and first thing in the morning. You don't stand a chance of getting a child to sleep through if you are still feeding her at night. It's much too great a comfort to miss out on!

SOLUTION:
THE CONTROLLED CRYING TECHNIQUE

If the wakefulness has settled into a regular pattern and is taking a severe toll on the family, you can try the Controlled Crying Technique. Versions of this technique are widely used by many sleep-trainers and family coaches, and I have always found it highly effective. In many cases, the technique will do the trick in less than a week.

At the outset, it is important to state that "controlled crying" is not the same as "leaving a child to cry." That old-fashioned remedy is not acceptable today; quite rightly, as it is both brutal and ineffective. "Controlled crying" is completely different. Unlike leaving a child to cry for long periods unattended, which reinforces a sense of abandonment, "controlled crying" demonstrates that you are still at hand, that you have not gone away, but that you are in charge and it's time to sleep.

I know that some parents don't want to leave their child crying for any length of time. While I wouldn't recommend the technique for every family, I do think it's one of the best ways of breaking a cycle of wakefulness.

The key to the technique is learning to distinguish between different types of cry. A high-pitched continuous cry or a low, groaning sound is the sign of a child in severe distress or pain. If your child is crying like that, it's time to act promptly and see what's the matter.

Crying for comfort or attention sounds different. It may begin with a whimper or a wail, but it tends to break off at intervals while the child waits for results, and then it returns. It's like a wave pattern. It's your job to observe and listen to your child's crying. Until you feel totally confident that you can recognize the different types of cry, don't start the technique.

This is how I use the technique:

★ The first time your child wakes, spend a few moments listening to the tone of the cry. Listen and observe. It's hard for any parent to have to listen to their child cry and not respond, but try to stay calm and don't allow yourself to be swamped by feelings of panic. If the crying does not indicate distress, wait a moment.

★ When there has been a sustained amount of crying, go to the child. Don't turn on the light. Don't make eye contact—look at the bridge of your child's nose or at his tummy. Don't talk or make conversation. Make a soothing noise—"sh" or "hush"—rub him on the back or the tummy, replace the covers and leave.

★ Accept the fact that your child will wake and cry again—it's a pattern you're dealing with. It might be an hour later, it might be five minutes later. When she cries again, wait for double the time before going into her and then repeat the same procedure.

★ On subsequent wakings, carry on doubling the intervals between going in to soothe him. This is the point when most parents find that the going gets tough. Let me tell you the emotions you're going to be feeling.

Responding to your child's cry is a natural
instinct. When you're trying to resist that
urge, you'll have a rush of adrenaline, your
hands will get hot and clammy, your heart
will pound, and you'll feel like you're losing
control. Understand that this is just your
body's natural reaction, and try to stay calm.
Get support from your partner or ask a friend
to stay with you overnight—someone who
can give you comfort and strength when
you're feeling like this.

★ Don't give up and don't let it slide. The
message will get across, perhaps sooner
than you think. You should begin to see
substantial improvements within a week.

PROBLEM:
GETTING OUT OF BED

Between two and three years, perhaps
younger, your child will discover she has
a secret weapon at her disposal: she can get
out of bed! Children who settle down to sleep
at a reasonable time and then repeatedly get
out of bed during the night are generally
looking for attention. They may give a variety
of reasons for their wakefulness—hunger,
thirst, nightmare, too hot, too cold—some
of which may be contradictory! The simple
fact, whatever they tell you, is that the
wakefulness has become a bad habit that
they know they can get away with.

SOLUTION:
THE STAYING IN BED TECHNIQUE

First of all, eliminate all possible excuses
for getting out of bed. Make sure there's a
glass of water beside the bed if your child
gets thirsty at night. Make sure she's had a
pee before she gets into bed. Give her fewer
and fewer things to get out of bed for.

If that doesn't work, use the Staying In
Bed Technique. Results are generally very
rapid with this technique. The key is not to
allow yourself to debate the reasons for the
wakefulness—the logic of the under-fives
being what it is, you won't win.

★ The first time the child gets out of bed, escort
him back and explain that it's bedtime. Give
him a little cuddle. Then leave.

★ The second time, put him back to bed and say,
"It's bedtime, darling." Give another cuddle
and leave.

★ The third time, put him back to bed without
saying a word.

★ Subsequent episodes should be treated in
the same way. No talking, no conversation,
no debate. You must get a grip on yourself
and understand your emotions. You are not
being mean, you are just teaching your
child to stay in bed.

★ It is very important with this technique
that the parent who put the child to bed in
the first place is the one who takes him back
to bed when he wakes up. Following through
is essential. This lets the child know that he
cannot play one parent against the other.

★ Use a star chart to reward your child for
a trouble-free night. Let him know that once
he has won a number of stars (no less than
three, no more than five), he can have a
reward for his behavior. But please be
sensible with your rewards! You don't want
to create more difficulties for yourself.

PROBLEM:
GETTING INTO YOUR BED

There's a huge difference of opinion on whether or not you should allow your kids to share your bed. For some, it's a natural, cosy part of family life. For others, it's their worst nightmare.

If your child is not well or is particularly insecure for some reason, then I don't see why she shouldn't have the comfort of your bed. Weekend mornings are good times for this type of closeness.

That's different from having your kids in bed with you every single night. At the risk of fanning the flames of controversy, I have to say I think that's a bad idea. Why?

★ You are unlikely to get a good night's sleep unless you, your partner and your child/children are all sound sleepers. Small children can occupy a disproportionate amount of bed space (often diagonally), and that's not even taking into account the wriggling and sudden desire for a chat at four in the morning. One minute, there'll be a sharp little elbow in your ribs, the next it's a little foot in your face. The squirming will carry on until you find yourself with 5% of the bed and 0% of the covers. Then your kid will fall asleep and you won't dare move. It's true, you may get more sleep, but that doesn't mean it's the right solution to that particular problem.

★ Parents need a private space to call their own. At the very least, this should be their own bed. A child in your bed is the most effective contraceptive there is. Becoming a parent doesn't mean you should have to say good-bye to intimacy or a sex life.

★ From my experience, it's dads who get the rawest deal. When a child slips into the parental bed, Dad often has to retreat to the living room sofa, the child's vacated bed, or, in extreme circumstances, the floor, just to get a decent night's sleep. If this goes on too long, your marriage will begin to show signs of strain.

★ Allow one child to get into bed with you, and you won't be able to say "no" to her brothers and sisters. It's the thin end of the wedge. In the same way, mothers who relax the "not in my bed" rule when their partners are away are storing up trouble for later.

★ Letting your child sleep with you is rarely a positive choice. In my experience, it's often a way of avoiding solving another problem.

SOLUTION:
THE CONTROLLED CRYING/STAYING IN BED TECHNIQUES

Which technique you choose will depend on the age of your child. If your toddler repeatedly wakes and cries in the night and you have been dealing with this problem by bringing him into bed with you, adopt the Controlled Crying Technique (see page 194). In the case of the persistent nighttime intruder, the older child who has got himself up and slipped into your bed, the Staying In Bed Technique (see opposite) works wonders. If your child has been getting into your bed regularly for the past five years, you're not necessarily going to break this pattern overnight.

PROBLEM:
NIGHTMARES AND NIGHT FEARS

All children occasionally suffer from nightmares and some develop a short-lived fear of the dark. Bad dreams and bouts of childhood illness go hand in hand, and nightmares, can also be associated with periods of stress and anxiety: the arrival of a new sibling, for example, or the first days settling in at nursery school. Often, however, there's no traceable cause. But there's a difference between the odd nightmare and the child who wakes up repeatedly night after night reporting a bad dream. In the latter case, it's probably a bad habit we're talking about.

SOLUTION:
SOOTHING/STAYING IN BED TECHNIQUE

In the case of a nightmare, go to the child or escort him back to his bed, soothe him and explain he has had a bad dream. Stay with him for a little while until the distress fades. Always take his fears seriously.

If a child develops a fear of the dark, nightlights in the bedroom and bathroom can be comforting. Leave the hall light on and the door ajar. Don't allow the child to persuade you to let her sleep with the light on. A favorite soft toy can be comforting.

Children who repeatedly use nightmares as an excuse for getting out of bed are probably trying to sneak around your defenses. For them, use the Staying In Bed Technique (page 196).

PROBLEM:
EARLY WAKING

Nine times out of ten, young children are raring to go much earlier in the morning than their parents. Children who have a natural sleeping pattern and who are put to bed at a time when they are tired, rather than over-tired, often wake up, if not at first light, then fairly soon afterwards. You may be hoping to snatch another half-hour's sleep, but your child has other ideas and is bouncing on your bed, letting you know all about them.

SOLUTION:
THE STAYING IN BED TECHNIQUE

As a parent of a young child, it is important to accept that long mornings in bed are a thing of the past for the time being. If your child is sleeping well, you should be getting adequate rest yourself and should be able to adjust your own schedule so that getting up earlier is not such a shock to the system. At the same time, there's early and there's the crack of dawn. If you have a real early bird on your hands, chances are you're not going to persuade her to go back to sleep. In this case, escort her back to bed, explain that it is too early, and tell her she can play quietly in bed or in her room until it is time for you to get up. This works a bit like the Staying In Bed Technique (page 196), in that you are limiting access to you at unacceptable times.

MY TOP TEN RULES

**TO SUM UP, HERE'S HOW MY TOP TEN RULES
APPLY TO SLEEPING PROBLEMS:**

1. PRAISE AND REWARDS

Praise each stage in the bedtime routine that is smoothly completed.
Praise children for their help and involvement. Single out something
to praise them for at the end of the day just before they go to sleep.

2. CONSISTENCY

Make sure that everyone involved in caring for your kids abides by the
same rules. Make sure that the parent who has put the child to bed is
the one who follows through if the child then wakes and gets up. It's
nice to let your kids snuggle up in bed with you on weekend mornings,
but don't allow your kids to get into bed with you on other occasions.

3. ROUTINE

Stick to the bedtime routine. Don't allow times to slip, and don't rush
things. Don't make exceptions to accommodate the TV schedule.

4. BOUNDARIES

A set bedtime and a set bedtime routine are clear boundaries that
tell your child that you are in charge. Making sure the child sleeps
through the night in her own bed spells out the same message.
These boundaries also make it clear that there are places and times
of the day reserved for you and your partner.

5. DISCIPLINE

Use the Sleep Separation Technique, the Controlled Crying Technique
and the Staying In Bed Technique to overcome sleep problems.

6. WARNINGS

Tell your child what comes next in the bedtime routine so he is mentally prepared for each stage. Set short time limits. Your aim is to be authoritative but not intimidating.

7. EXPLANATIONS

Keep explanations and debates to a minimum when settling children who have awakened in the night. The first two times, explain that "It's bedtime" and after that, say nothing.

8. RESTRAINT

Don't become so overwhelmed by the sound of your child crying that you rush in to comfort her every two minutes. Keep the emotional temperature down as much as possible.

9. RESPONSIBILITY

Get your kids involved in their own bedtime, by setting them small achievable tasks—undressing, pulling out the bath plug, fetching a toy for a sibling.

10. RELAXATION

Bedtime and the time leading up to bedtime should be a period of calm. Baths and bedtime stories help a child unwind. And once you've got a good sleeping pattern established for your child, make the most of the rest of the evening and relax yourself!

Quality time

In an ideal world, every minute you spend with your family should be quality time. In the real world, it's not going to work out exactly like that. Bringing up kids is rewarding, but it's also hard work.

You need to take every opportunity you can to turn that work into fun. If you set boundaries in place and back them up, you'll start to enjoy your kids rather than see them as a chore to be dealt with. Enjoyment is important. This is a precious period, even if it doesn't always seem that way, and it will be over all too quickly.

Quality time also means that each person in the family should get what they need—Mom, Dad, older brothers and sisters, as well as young children. That takes a bit of juggling and planning so that everyone gets individual attention as well as time off.

When you're a parent and your mental, emotional and physical purse is empty, you won't be able to hand out loose change to anyone else. There's a fine line between doing the right thing and being a martyr. If you don't look after yourself and your relationship, everything else is going to suffer in the long run.

In our parents' or grandparents' day, it was rare for both parents to work, and single-parent households were not that common. Today, both types of family are on the increase. That's just a fact of life. Working mothers and single parents come in for a lot of criticism in the media. Ignore it. Just as you shouldn't set your child up for failure, don't set yourself up for blame and guilt. Get the support you need, use it, and relax.

Getting support

A lot of the stress associated with parenting comes from unrealistic expectations. There's no such thing as a perfect parent. And whatever any other mom or dad might tell you, there's no such thing as a perfect child. Some people are always boasting about their kids and what they can do and how early they did it. Don't let that make you feel inadequate. If those same parents were completely truthful, they'd let you in on the problems they're keeping to themselves.

In the old days, when people didn't move around as much as they do today, most families lived close to a natural support network of friends and relatives, people whom they trusted and had known all their lives. Parents may not have relied on the paid services of babysitters or nannies, but that doesn't mean Aunt Edith or Grandma wasn't called upon from time to time to take up the slack.

You can't do it alone. Getting support is not a sign of failure, it's a sign of strength. Parenting is an enormous organizational job, whether you're a working parent or not. Everyone needs to rely on other people from time to time for support.

You don't just need support at obvious crisis times—when you're going to be in hospital having a new baby, for example, or on moving day. You need it as a matter of course. Parents should not give up their identities and outside interests just because children have come along. Both parents need time to do things for themselves, and time to be together as adults.

Find a babysitter you can trust and rely on. Set up a babysitting circle with other families who have small children. Ask your mom down for the weekend. We may not live in such close-knit communities these days, but there are still plenty of ways to put a support group in place.

Look after yourself

In a paid job, you'd expect a bonus once in a while, maybe even a promotion. In the same way, you should give yourself a monthly treat—a massage, a haircut, a trip to the cinema, a shopping trip, a meal in a restaurant, an evening with friends. You have needs just like everyone else in the household, and unless you look after them, you're going to be running on empty. Quality time is not an optional extra. It's a necessity.

The early months can be a particular time of adjustment, with plenty of highs and lows. Recognize that you need to look after yourself, as postnatal depression can creep up on you.

If you were an athlete, you'd expect to train for your event. You'd watch your diet. If you had an important meeting or presentation at work, you'd prepare ahead of time. Being a parent is an important role and you shouldn't neglect your physical, mental, or emotional well-being. You shouldn't be putting up with sleep deprivation; you shouldn't allow yourself to become housebound and isolated. You shouldn't find it impossible to read the paper or curl up with a book. Although you will definitely make many sacrifices, parenting is not about martyrdom. It's about meeting needs, including your own.

If this is important for a parent who has given up work to look after children, it's doubly important for a single working mom or dad. Don't allow yourself to be so tortured with guilt about not staying home with the kids that you give up any idea of looking after yourself or having your own life. You've got a babysitter, nanny, or family member who's looking after the kids—or maybe they're in school—and they are getting what they need. You're spending quality time with them when you come home from work and on the weekends. But you also need time for yourself so you can keep on an even keel.

Individual attention

One of the key functions of a daily routine, aside from setting fixed times for meals and bed, is to juggle your schedule so that each child in your family has individual attention from both Mom and Dad. This can be done very easily by taking turns with the bedtime routine. One night, it's Dad's turn to put the six-year-old to bed and Mom's turn to bath the toddler and settle her down. The next night, it's the other way around. On the weekend, you can also vary who does what. Mom takes the eleven-year-old out on a shopping trip, while Dad and the four-year-old wash the car together. Think of ways of mixing it up so that you aren't always stuck in the same roles all the time.

Very demanding small children have a habit of stealing the limelight from their older brothers and sisters, who may not even complain. Don't mistake a lack of protest for acceptance. Older kids need your attention, too. They need help with homework, a chance to talk over what's happened at school, advice, and support. They can tie their shoelaces and run their own baths, but they still need you in lots of ways. One-on-one attention from both parents is essential, and it should be equal to the attention you pay to your younger kids.

Sibling rivalry

One of the great enemies of quality time is sibling rivalry. It happens in practically every family. A common age gap between children is two years. It's not up to me to tell you how to space your children, but it's important to be aware that the two-year gap can result in a more intense form of sibling rivalry than a gap of three or four years. At three or four, your older child will still be jealous, but you will have a better chance of dealing with it because he will be able to understand more than a child who's in the throes of toddlerhood.

PREPARING FOR THE CHANGE

Your child may not know that your fast-disappearing waistline means a baby is on the way, but she may well have picked up on subtle changes before you even tell her that she's going to have a new baby brother or sister. It might be simply that you're more tired than usual, or feeling sick.

If your child notices your expanding tummy and asks about it, use that as the opportunity to tell her the news so you can start to prepare her for the new addition to your family. Otherwise, let it go until you're about six months along. Time passes very slowly for little kids—three months is enough time to prepare her, but not such a long time for her to wait.

Let your child feel your bump. Let him feel the baby kicking. Don't go overboard and build up the new arrival too much. Most small children would rather have you to themselves than share attention with a new baby brother or sister. Instead of telling him how much he's going to love his new sibling, let him know that he's going to be a big brother and a big help to you. Keep talking about what you're going to do together after the birth. It may sound strange, but many small children think that a new baby is a replacement, not an addition. When a child gets anxious about a new arrival, he's thinking: "What's going to happen to me? Am I still going to live here?"

Your child may have lots of questions about the mechanics of birth. Don't give her more information than she can handle, and don't tell her anything that might make her worry about you.

THE BIG DAY . . .

Arrange for your child to be looked after by someone he knows and trusts while you are in hospital. It can be hard to get the timing right—you may have a few false alarms—but put a flexible plan in place and tell your child what's going to be happening. Lay in a few presents. Buy him a "Big Boy" congratulation card.

The first time you see the child after the birth, make a real fuss of her. The whole point is to make her feel completely involved. She'll have missed you, she might have been worried, and she'll be overwhelmed with emotion. It's a big step. Give her a present and pay her a lot of attention. Don't be so absorbed with the baby that you barely notice her at all. Let her hold the baby. Give her lots of praise. This is not a time to introduce your child to the notion of equal attention. At this moment, as far as she's concerned, it should be all about her.

. . . AND AFTER

One of the ways in which children reveal jealousy is by acting up at those times when you have to pay attention to your younger child. For a jealous toddler, negative attention for doing something unspeakable is better than no attention at all.

The Involvement Technique (see page 76) replaces the negative attention with positive attention by getting your child involved with what you're doing. Ask him to help pass you things and praise him for it. Keep talking. Explain what you're doing. Notice his good behavior. With the Involvement Technique, the older child is getting attention at the same time as the baby.

Many kids regress a little when a new brother or sister arrives. They might start talking baby talk again, wetting the bed, or generally start to behave younger than their age. The Involvement Technique can be a good way of making sure that this stage is short-lived. Give your child plenty of praise for being a "big girl." That way she won't think there's so much mileage in trying to turn back the clock.

SHARED PLAY

Two toddlers aren't going to be able to share or play together. If you have two small children who are close in age, there will be a stage when you will be spending most of your time separating them, diverting them, and otherwise stopping them from bashing each other over the head.

When your kids are a little older, you can introduce "shared play." Get your older child to help choose and run games, so she thinks she's in charge. Encourage her to behave better by giving her a little bit of responsibility. Ask her to show her little brother how to play a game or play with a toy.

CONSTANT FIGHTING

Try to ignore low-level skirmishes. Kids learn to sort things out for themselves if you aren't always running to the rescue. Don't try to find out "who started it" or who was to blame. If they're fighting, they're both at fault.

If one child lashes out at the other and if there is real aggressive behavior, take action immediately. Use the Naughty Step Technique (see page 80), or the One-Strike-And-You're-Out Technique (page 84) if that doesn't work. Make it clear that you won't tolerate harmful or hurtful behavior.

COUPLE TIME

On *Supernanny*, I set "homework" for a couple who hadn't spent an evening on their own since the birth of their toddler, two and a half years before. That homework was to go out for the evening. Two years is a long time for a couple to go without any quality time of their own. Relationships need to be looked after, which means you need to spend adult time together talking about other things, not the kids. Go away for the weekend by yourselves once in a while. Drop the kids off to spend the night with friends, and spend the evening at home by yourselves if you don't want to go out. That's not selfish or negligent, it's an important way of reminding yourself why you're together in the first place.

Parents who regularly spend quality time on their own and with each other find it much easier to be consistent in their approach to their kids. They find it natural to present a united front, because the lines of communication are always open and they are still functioning as a couple and not just as Mom and Dad. It also makes it easier to find a way of sharing the burden of care so that it's not just one parent managing the bedtime routine every night, it's a shared task. Resentments build up when one parent is overloaded—"I've been putting them to bed for a week now!"—and that's also when inconsistencies can start to creep in. If that kind of situation carries on, parents can find themselves acting out their differences by handling their kids in very different ways, and that will only make things worse.

FAMILY FUN

Make time to have fun together as a family. It can be an outing,
it can be a picnic in the garden. It can be a holiday at the seaside,
or a wet Sunday afternoon playing a board game. Forget about the
chores for once—they'll get done. When you look back in years to
come—you won't remember the fact that you didn't change the
beds one week, you'll remember that special day flying kites in the
park.

Enjoy your children!

MY TOP TEN RULES

TO SUM UP, HERE'S HOW MY TOP TEN RULES APPLY TO QUALITY TIME:

1. PRAISE AND REWARDS

Praise and attention are the best rewards. But do treat your child to a special present and card when a new brother or sister comes along. It will really help him feel involved.

2. CONSISTENCY

Parents are likely to find it easier to be consistent when they have enough time together as a couple. Make sure you get away for the odd weekend together and have regular nights off.

3. ROUTINE

Arrange your routine so that every child has one-on-one attention from each parent every day. Make these "special" times. Work out a rotation so that parents also share chores.

4. BOUNDARIES

Children must learn to respect the fact that you need quality time for yourself and as a couple. Clear rules about behavior help to prevent excessive sibling rivalry.

5. DISCIPLINE

Back up your rules with discipline if necessary. Use the Naughty Step Technique for aggressive behavior or constant fighting. Be prepared to separate warring toddlers.

6 WARNINGS

A verbal warning is an essential part of discipline. It allows the child the chance to correct her own behavior. Don't rush to discipline a child for aggression or fighting without giving a warning first.

7 EXPLANATIONS

Prepare your child for the arrival of a new family member. Give her plenty of reassurance, but don't give her so much information that she starts to worry.

8. RESTRAINT

Don't overreact to every skirmish. Let children sort some things out for themselves, providing they are at no risk of hurting themselves or each other.

9. RESPONSIBILITY

Use the Involvement Technique to ease jealousy. Give lots of praise. Allow older children to plan games for the little ones.

10. RELAXATION

Don't allow yourself to get run-down or overloaded. Get support and look after yourself as a matter of course. Make time for family fun.

USEFUL CONTACTS

Following is a list of websites for expecting parents and parents of young children.

www.adoption.com Parents of adopted children may face special challenges and this website offers information, support, and advice on how to successfully prepare for the challenges. There are sections that prepare parents for the "waiting period," suggestions for including your extended family in the process, and guidance on when and how to answer questions your young child may one day have about his adoption.

www.babycenter.com This website helps you chart your baby's development in utero, while preparing you for the first few years of parenting. Viewers can customize their webpage to receive information specific to their needs, and receive a free weekly newsletter featuring current articles about pregnancy and birthing. There is also a section where viewers can log on and chat with other mothers about general issues, or arrange to meet up with expectant moms in your region.

www.brandnewdad.com Is the new mom getting all the attention? Looking for a website devoted to the special, sometimes neglected issues of coping with new fatherhood? Brandnewdad.com offers practical advice for new and expectant fathers. Compare your feelings and issues to those of others in the online community section where people might write in on being an "older" dad, how to calm a crying baby, or financial planning issues. A month by month guide to your baby's first year will also quell any questions dads may have about their child's development.

www.childdevelopmentinfo.com Recommended by *Psychology Today* magazine and the *American Psychological Association,* this award-winning site focuses on issues of child development. Different sections of the site educate viewers about physical and emotional growth of young children, parenting tips for raising toddlers, information on early signs of learning disorders, news and guidelines regarding the media and children, and ways to improve your young child's learning capabilities.

www.ehow.com The general eHow website offers instructions on how to do anything. Just plug in your parenting question and wait for an answer. How to prepare siblings for a new baby, how best to position your infant for nursing, or how to easily put your baby down for a nap can all be answered on this site.

www.essortment.com/in/Children.Infants.Toddlers/index.htm PageWise is a section of this website that attempts to "mine all the knowledge of the human race and make it available for free . . . ." The Family and Parenting index includes topics on all aspects of infancy and childhood, and includes articles from experts on care and feeding of newborns, developmental toys and games for babies and toddlers, new theories of parenting (such as attachment parenting), children's health, diapering, discipline, infant massage, baby's first shoes, what the Apgar test means, and many other topics.

www.divorceinfo.com/parentingissues.htm This informational website on divorce features a section that discusses pivotal parenting issues that make or break a child's transition when parents are divorcing. Custody guides, rules for crisis management, and raising responsible kids in the face of instability are included in a non-judgmental compassionate discussion.

www.family.go.com Disney Online's *Family Fun* magazine has a website that is mainly devoted to activities, crafts, and field trips you can take with your children. The parenting section features an interesting health page that discusses alternative medicine options for dealing with dental care, the immune system, and stress levels for children who have difficulty coping with a fast-paced educational environment.

www.familyeducation.com Divided into age groups, this website includes tips on nutrition, sports and fitness, and entertainment ideas for holidays. Downloads include educational materials for math and reading from pre-K up to 12th grade. Learning differences and how to spot potential problems are also discussed, and articles on social aspects of early childhood can be found.

www.fathersdirect.com Get tips from other dads on how to connect with your pregnant partner, and learn the blow by blow of what actually happens in the birthing room and how you can contribute to the health of your unborn child through articles or the discussions and Dadtalk sections of the website.

www.forbes.com/execpicks/2004/07/19/cz_lk_0719parents.html This informative article clues new parents in on the realities of budgeting for growing families.

www.4woman.gov The website of the National Women's Health Information Center gives nutritional information for pregnant women including the amounts of vitamins needed on a daily basis. It also includes links to other nutrition websites and what diets to follow for women whose health is compromised.

www.health.yahoo.com/health/centers/parenting The search engine company has an entire section of their website devoted to the health of your children and how to navigate the seemingly endless array of topics and questions that may arise in your home. Subjects are varied and cover a vast range of material, from how to calm your child if she needs to have blood drawn to bath time fears of young toddlers. Many articles discuss ideas you may be reluctant to bring up with your pediatrician for fear of being labeled "overprotective." Useful information will help you evaluate whether or not to seek further guidance with a medical professional.

www.iparenting.com Iparenting.com is an online community for parents to become part of in whatever way they choose. Looking for health and fitness information for your toddler? Maybe you'd like to think of activities your child's grandparents would be comfortable spearheading. Perhaps you'd like to share stories of your child's birth or early years. With its chatty style, wide-ranging array of topics, and celebrity moms and dads of the month, iparenting.com is perfect for surfing while your baby is napping.

www.kidsource.com Up-to-the-minute information about all types of recalls affecting kids is a valuable component of this website featuring educational and healthcare information for parents of kids of all ages. Book reviews and tips of the day round out a long list of topics concerning your child's safety and welfare.

www.kidsgrowth.com This health site was developed by pediatricians for parents and takes a whole, progressive approach to kids' health and parenting. Articles cover both traditional and timely topics, and many focus on cultural factors that influence our children's well-being and quality of life. Topics range from back pain in children to the effects of television advertising to hidden sources of poisonous carbon monoxide in your home.

www.mothering.com The online site of *Mothering Magazine,* this organization celebrates natural mothering and family living. For parents who advocate a "greener," more organic lifestyle for their child, articles on schools and environment, natural first aid, prenatal testing, and kids and the media will provide useful information and support.

www.pbs.org/parents In Spanish and English, PBSParents, an arm of the Public Broadcasting Station, provides parents with tips on early learning, child development, and creative expression. Age-appropriate books are recommended and reviewed in addition to advice on how to talk to kids about difficult issues, helping children make sense of different forms of media, and strategies for turning your child into an avid reader.

www.newparentsnetwork.org Available in English or Spanish language, the New Parents Network gathers important and helpful information on all aspects of childrearing from the experts themselves. Contributions to the site from the Centers for Disease Control, American Academy of Pediatrics, the Environmental Protection Agency, Recalls.gov, and others cover a timely array of topics vital to your child's health and welfare. Articles are clearly titled and easy for the layperson to understand. Categories include car safety, diseases and disabilities, recalled children's products, pregnancy, childbirth, newborns, safety and poison control, child care and education, and support services for parents and caregivers.

www.netsmartz.com Netsmartz.com is an invaluable resource for parents whose young children are ready to start using the computer and Internet. The site helps teach parents and children about possible dangers children may encounter online and how to navigate the different software available for child-proofing your computer.

www.parents-talk.com ParentsTalk is a general website featuring information on newborns, toddlers, grade-schoolers, step-parenting, and gift and party ideas for kids. A fun feature of the site are the message boards connecting parents to an online community where all sorts of questions are asked and answered, and all topics of parenting are discussed.

www.parenting.com The website of *Parenting* magazine covers topics from

pregnancy and early childhood to how to maintain your identity as a mom. The baby and child sections are well organized into topics of development, health, care, eating, behavior, activities, and lifestyle. Downloads include growth charts where you can personalize and chart your own child's progress. Timely health alerts and information are featured prominently to keep you informed about issues your pediatrician may neglect to mention at regular checkups.

www.parentsplace.com Expecting parents and parents of newborns will find a wealth of information pertaining to those early weeks and months of a newborn's life including information on topics such as breastfeeding, teething, colic, and sleep patterns.

www.parentsoup.com This comprehensive website is the winner of several national consumer website awards and features a "soup to nuts" approach to parenting topics. Sleep training, potty training, budgeting, fertility, and working mom issues are all tackled with thoughtful advice and a nod toward understanding that what works in theory is sometimes difficult to implement in practice.

www.postpartum.net This website of the Postpartum Support International organization gives new mothers suffering from postpartum symptoms information on how to cope. Articles may be directed to mothers, fathers, and extended family members, all offering support for a woman suffering from this mood disorder.

www.preemie-1.org For parents of premature babies, this website is devoted to offering information and suggestions on how to get through the difficult early days of shock and worry. Lists of questions to ask your neonatologist, practical suggestions on how to cope with being unable to bring your newborn home from the hospital, and input from other parents in the same position provide support for parents of preemies. The site also contains a list of reading materials and other links for information.

www.pta.org The website of the National Parent Teacher Association, a child advocacy organization, gives parents information on child development and education. Articles featured cover self-esteem issues and positive discipline. Information on how to evaluate community schools and forming relationships with educators can also be found.

www.responsiblekids.net Looking for information on breastfeeding, or maybe on immunization of infants, or even how to

manage as a single parent? This website will send you to links for a wide variety of important topics. Parents of special needs children may find the list of online resources for children with learning differences especially helpful.

www.saferchild.org Safer Child, Inc., is a non-profit organization with a website containing up-to-date safety information for young children. The all-inclusive index of topics covers subjects from talking to your children about terrorism and car safety seats to dehydration and ear infections. Each topic has its own links to more comprehensive and specific information.

www.sesameworkshop.org From the folks who brought you *Sesame Street,* the Sesame Workshop website is also devoted to educating children and parents through the celebration of imagination. In addition to arts and crafts or field trip ideas, parents can read how to ready toddlers for school, answer their most probing questions, and help them segue through the different stages of early childhood with a bit more ease.

www.thenewparentsguide.com Get information on parenting and shopping for baby, new baby checklist needs, and product buying guides. A special section on family travel helps you navigate destinations and hotels that are family friendly.

www.totcity.com If your toddler wants to play on Mommy's computer, this is the perfect site to visit with him. Online games and activities with an educational emphasis will hold your child's interest. Familiar characters from educational television and books can be found on the TotCity Arcade page.

www.urbanbaby.com If you live in a major metropolitan area of the United States and need to connect with other mothers, this is the website for you. Although full of resources guides, offline event calendars, and up to date information on health news, what really draws viewers to this site are the message boards and chat rooms. Parents (mostly moms) discuss everything from the difficulty of staying close to your spouse during the early years of child rearing to how to confront another mom about their child's aggression. Message boards are arranged in categories from fertility issues to finding playgroups, and for those who are tired of parenting issues, political and current event issues of the day are also up for discussion.

INDEX